Sampler Book 7, Ontario in Colour Photos, Saving Our History One Photo at a Time

Photography by Barbara Raué ©2018

Series Name: Cruising Ontario

Sampling from several towns

Each photo I take that precedes a demolition, or a natural disaster such as a tornado or a fire, is meeting this aim of mine of Saving Our History One Photo at a Time. There are more than 100 towns already photographed which you can visit without moving from a comfortable chair in your living room. ©All the photos in this book have been taken with my cameras. I own the rights to them. I confirm that I will never submit any content for which I do not have the exclusive publishing rights. I will adhere to all terms in the Content Guidelines when publishing new content.

Cover: 31 Lakeshore Drive, Morrisburg

Table of Contents

Mariatown to Maitland Ontario – My Top 8 Picks

Morrisburg, Ontario – My Top 11 Picks

Brockville, Ontario – My Top 12 Picks

Merrickville, Ontario – My Top 16 Picks

Smiths Falls, Ontario – My Top 8 Picks

Portland and Newboro, Ontario – My Top 12 Picks

Westport and Port Elmsley, Ontario – My Top 5 Picks

Perth, Ontario – My Top 15 Picks

Mariatown to Maitland Ontario – My Top 8 Picks

Mariatown and Iroquois

South Dundas is a municipality in eastern Ontario in the United Counties of Stormont, Dundas and Glengarry along the north shore of the St. Lawrence River. It is located about sixty miles/one hundred kilometers south of Ottawa. The township was created on January 1, 1998, by amalgamating the former townships of Matilda and Williamsburg with the villages of Iroquois and Morrisburg. Mariatown is located in the township.

The McIntosh apple was discovered and cultivated in South Dundas near Williamsburg. John McIntosh moved to Upper Canada in 1796. In 1811 he acquired a farm in Dundela, and while clearing the land of second growth discovered several apple seedlings. He transplanted these, and one bore the superior fruit which became famous as the McIntosh Red apple. John's son Allan established a nursery and promoted this new species extensively.

Morrisburg and Iroquois were partially flooded by the creation of the St. Lawrence Seaway in 1958. Unlike the Lost Villages of Cornwall and Osnabruck Townships, the two towns were relocated to higher ground in the same area.

An artificial lake, Lake Saint Lawrence, now extends from a hydroelectric dam at Cornwall to the control structure at Iroquois, and replaces the formerly narrow and turbulent section of river that was impassable to large vessels.

Cardinal

Edwardsburgh/Cardinal is a township in the United Counties of Leeds and Grenville of eastern Ontario. Edwardsburgh Township was surveyed in 1783. The Township of Edwardsburgh/Cardinal was formed on January 1, 2001, through the amalgamation of Edwardsburgh Township with the Village of Cardinal. It is a historical community with many old homes and buildings, including one-room school houses, grist mills, and churches. It is situated along the St. Lawrence River and extends back into rural hamlets. The South Nation River passes through the township. The township's main population centres are Cardinal, Johnstown, and Spencerville.

Ten percent of the area's water drains into the St. Lawrence, while ninety percent drains into the South Nation River. The flow of the South Nation River through this area is very sluggish with poor drainage, due to the fact there is little drop in elevation along the river; this leads to the formation of bogs and swamps, and also makes the area prone to seasonal flooding.

Up until the 18th century, the land was covered with thick, mature, mixed forests. The original forest was almost completely cleared throughout the years and the forest that stands today is mostly secondary growth over previously cleared land. The forests in the area presently contain numerous types of deciduous oak, birch, ash and maple trees. The common coniferous trees in the area include many types of pine and cedar as well as balsam fir and white spruce. In the darker, acidic soils around the bogs and swamps there are tamarack trees, as well as juniper and black spruce.

In 1673, the French, working with native tribes from the area, built a storehouse on Old Breeches River, now known as Johnstown Creek. This storehouse was used to hold supplies for upriver trading posts such as Fort Frontenac (now Kingston). In 1759, The French settlers built Fort de Levis on Chimney Island, in the St. Lawrence River just off of Johnstown, between it and Ogdensburg. The purpose of this fort was to protect the St. Lawrence River from the British. It was captured by Major-General Jeffrey Amherst in August 1760 during the Battle of the Thousand Islands. The island on which the fort once stood was permanently flooded during the construction of the St. Lawrence Seaway.

Johnstown

Before the construction of dams and later the Seaway, Johnstown was fronted by a calm section of the St. Lawrence River located between two rapids. By 1784, Loyalists were residing in the township and until 1790 the landing point and base camp for these settlers was at Johnstown.

Johnstown is part of the township of Edwardsburgh/Cardinal in the United Counties of Leeds and Grenville in eastern Ontario. It is located at the Canadian terminus of the Ogdensburg-Prescott International Bridge.

In 1792 John Graves Simcoe, the first Lieutenant Governor of Upper Canada, established himself in Johnstown which then became the district's administrative seat. This led to the court of quarter sessions (the district's government) alternating its meeting location between Johnstown and Cornwall, and to the construction of a courthouse and gaol. The courthouse was a log structure, which stood near the present site of the Prescott-Ogdensburg Bridge. By the late 1790s, the village was also home to a sawmill, gristmill, and an inn and tavern. Census records indicate by 1807, there were thirty-six houses and a general store. In 1808, the Seat of Justice was moved to Elizabethtown (now Brockville), as it was a more central location in the district.

New Wexford is located in Edwardsburgh/Cardinal Township, in the United Counties of Leeds and Grenville of eastern Ontario.

Prescott

Prescott is a small town located on the north shore of the Saint Lawrence River in the United Counties of Leeds and Grenville. Colonel Edward Jessup remained loyal to the British during the revolutionary war. He was granted 1,000 acres and in 1810 had building lots surveyed for the town which he named in honor of General Robert Prescott who had been Governor-in-Chief of Canada between 1797 and 1807.

Prescott was a strategic military site for the protection of the Canadian border against American and French invasions. Fort Wellington was built in 1812 to defend the St. Lawrence River and the town. Prescott is located at the head of the St. Lawrence rapids. Before the completion of the canals between here and Montreal in 1847, Prescott was the eastern terminus of Great Lakes navigation.

Established in 1810, it became a center for the forwarding, or shipping, trade and an important center in Montreal's commercial system. One of the earliest forwarders at Prescott was Captain William Gilkison who began operations in 1811. The population of Upper Canada increased rapidly after 1820; the trade expanded and forwarding firms, including Henderson & Hooker, and Macpherson, Crane & Co., established ship building yards, wharves, and warehouses along the waterfront. The forwarding trade flourished before the building of railways and canals. The railway came in 1854.

During four days in November 1838, British troops and local militia defeated an invasion force of 300 American hunters and Canadian rebels. The Battle of the Windmill victory prevented the invasion force from capturing Fort Wellington in Prescott and cutting the St. Lawrence communications link, which would have left Upper Canada open to invasion.

By 1887, in addition to the fort, barracks, and military hospital, there were twenty-three hotels, twenty-four taverns, a distillery, two breweries, two foundries, two tanneries, two potters, a bank, a saw mill, a quarry, a brick factory, a shipyard, a grain elevator, and a farmers' market building.

With a town of 3,000 people, smaller establishments and services were also present: a bowling alley, a theatre, several newspapers, a telegraph office, bakeries, general merchants, doctors' offices, a dentist, a library, a college, two schools, four churches, many docks and wharves with large storage buildings, and a ferry service to Ogdensburg, New York.

Maitland

Maitland is a small village in the United Counties of Leeds and Grenville. It is located along the St. Lawrence River about five kilometers east of the City of Brockville. Loyalists began to settle the area in the late 1700s and into the early 19th century by building homesteads, establishing businesses and opening small factories. During the early part of the century, Maitland was on the opposite end of a supply route running to Merrick's Mills, which aided in its growth; the construction of the Welland Canal and other canal systems through the St. Lawrence allowed goods to be transported to and from the village. A wharf was used for collecting goods, and many mills were constructed.

One of Maitland's most notable landmarks was constructed in 1828: the Longley Tower, which was originally built as a windmill along the St. Lawrence River. The tower had a brief life as a windmill, but it did not generate enough power to sustain anything for long; it was later converted into a distillery. Longley imported a steam engine from Europe, built a flour mill, and constructed a stone building out of which he ran a general store and post office. Major Charles Lemon constructed two mills, a foundry, and a blacksmith shop to serve the village.

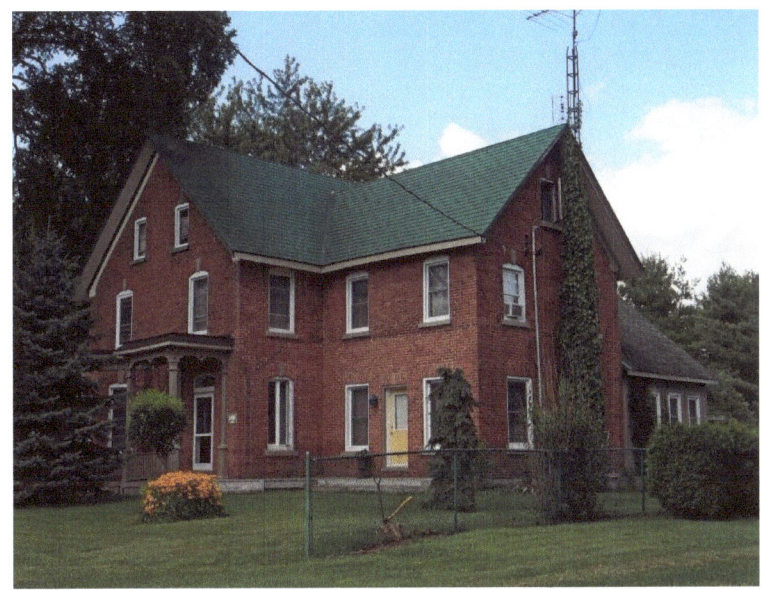

Mariatown - Gothic – gable roof, voussoirs with keystones

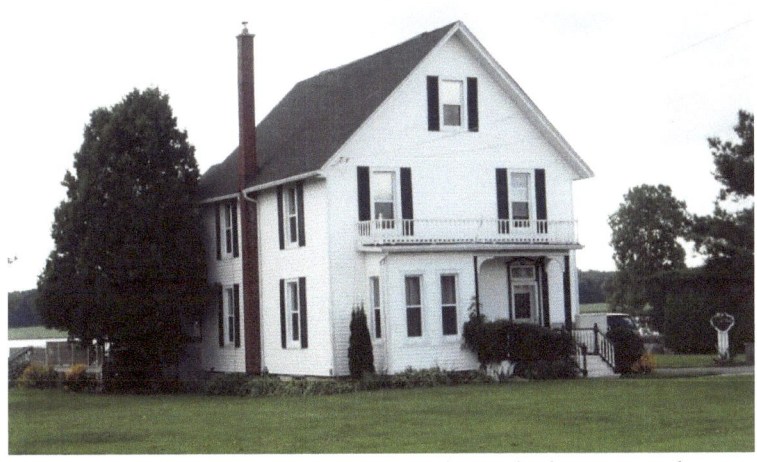

Mariatown - 2½ storeys, second floor balcony with open railing above rectangular bay window and open porch

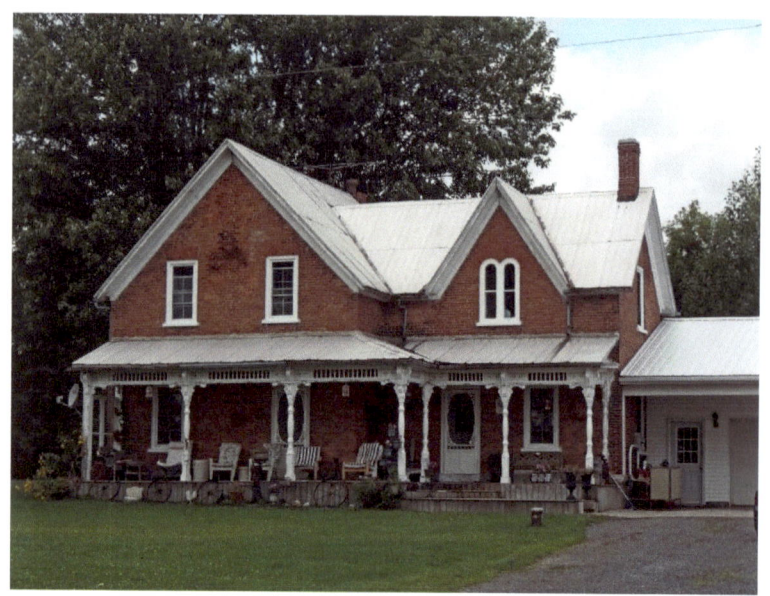

Iroquois - Victorian - decorative veranda support posts, no railing

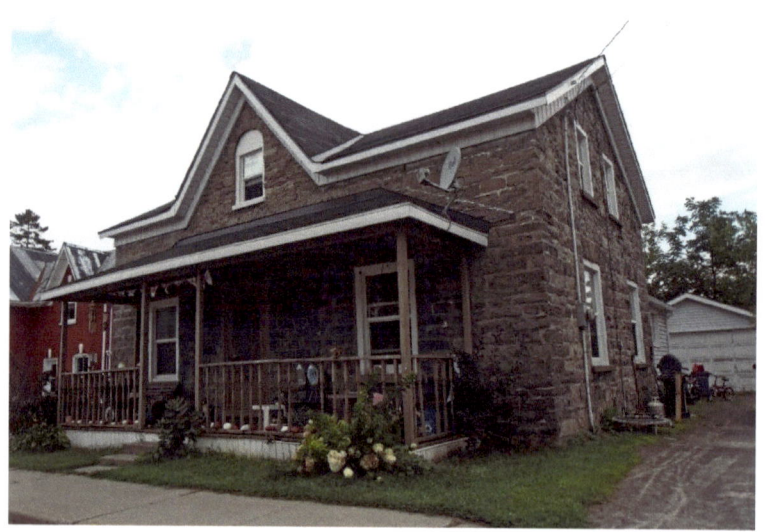

Cardinal - Gothic – stone

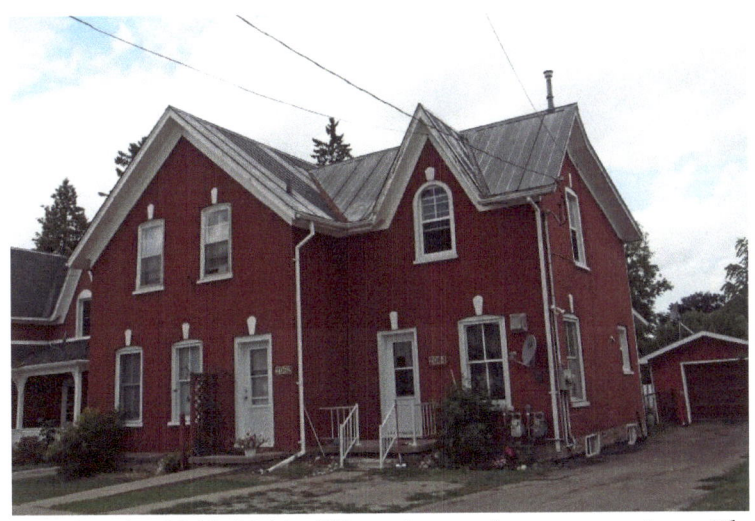

Cardinal - 2062-2064 - Victorian style – voussoirs with keystones

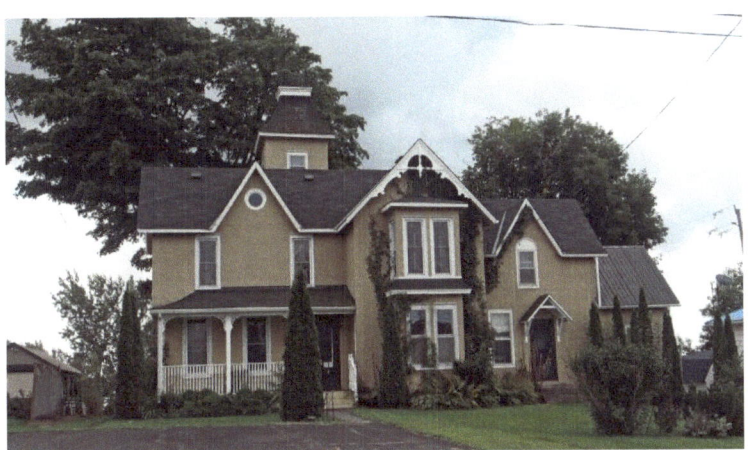

Cardinal - Victorian – semi-circular spindle decoration on gable above two-storey rectangular bay windows; three-storey tower with iron cresting on top; decorative veranda support posts, open railing

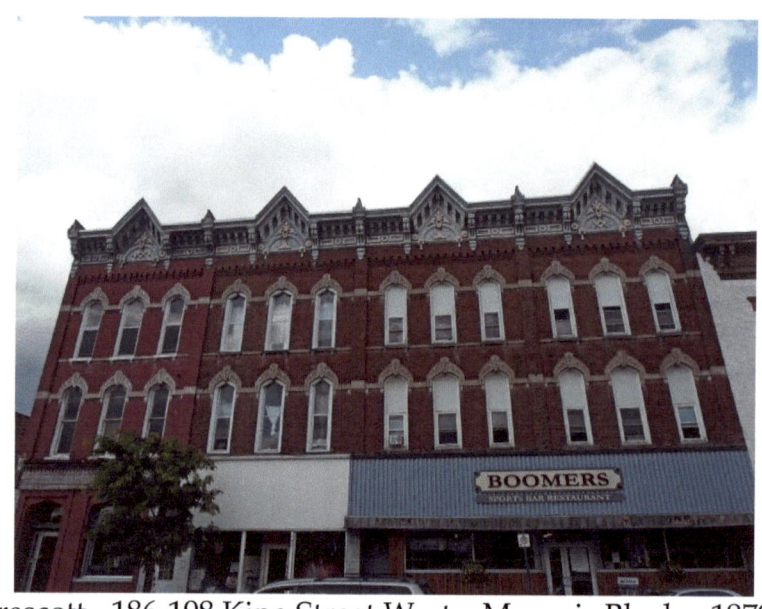

Prescott - 186-198 King Street West – Masonic Block – 1879 - building is composed of four sections three storeys high; arched windows with cornices and keystones decorated with linear designs; cornice brackets, beveled dentil molding; over the central bay of each section is a symbol of the Masonic Order

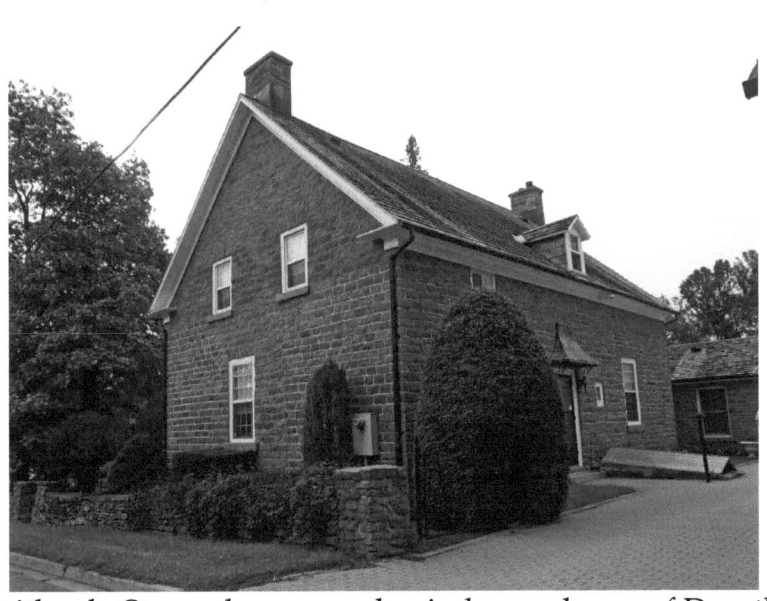

Maitland - Stone, dormer, sash windows – home of Dorothy Martha Dumbrille, novelist, poet, historian, author of ten books – During World War II she wrote a novel, *All This Difference*, which addressed the tensions between the French Canadian inhabitants and the early Scots living in Glengarry County. This house, her ancestral home, was the setting of a subsequent novel, *Deep Doorways*, published in 1947.

Morrisburg, Ontario – My Top 11 Picks

In 1997, Morrisburg was amalgamated with the Village of Iroquois, Matilda and Williamsburg Townships into the Township of South Dundas, in the United Counties of Stormont, Dundas and Glengarry along the north shore of the St. Lawrence River. The county was named in 1792 to honour Henry Dundas, who was Lord Advocate for Scotland and Colonial Secretary at the time. Matilda and Williamsburgh were two of Upper Canada's original eight Royal Townships.

On November 11, 1813, the Battle of Crysler's Farm, at which a British force repelled an invading American army, took place near here. United Empire Loyalists settled in Dundas County creating West Williamsburg; it was part of the Williamsburg Canal project. Between 1843 and 1856, canals were built on the north side of the St. Lawrence River. West Williamsburg was renamed Morrisburg in 1851 in honour of Brockville politician, James Morris, who was the first Postmaster General of the United Provinces of Canada. By 1860, Morrisburg had a growing manufacturing base consisting of a gristmill, a carding mill and a fanning mill. The Grand Trunk Railroad reached Morrisburg in 1855. A hydroelectric power plant was built in 1901.

During the 1950s, portions of Morrisburg were relocated because of expected flooding which would occur with the St. Lawrence Seaway project. Over eighty homes were moved and the entire downtown business district was demolished and relocated in a shopping plaza. The Canadian National Railway line was moved about a kilometre north of its original location. Much of the former rail bed was used for reconstructing Highway 2. Buildings and other artefacts were moved and assembled to create Upper Canada Village, a tribute to the area's pioneers.

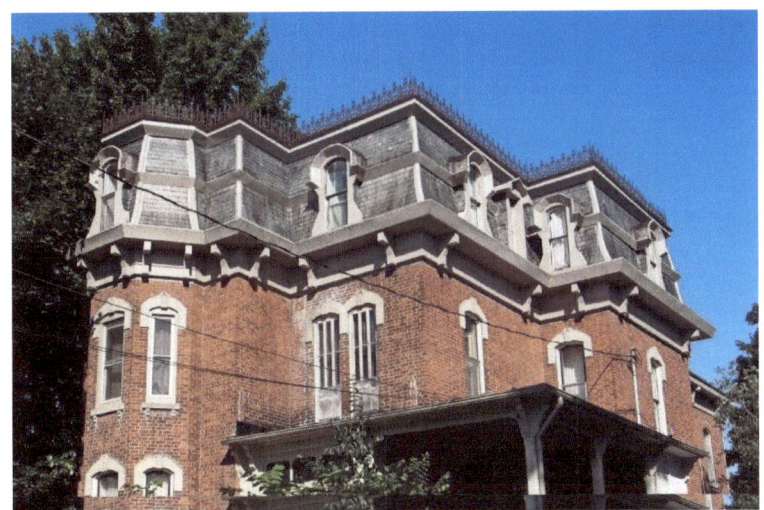

22 Lakeshore Drive – Second Empire – built 1879 – mansard roof, rounded dormers, heavy cornice brackets

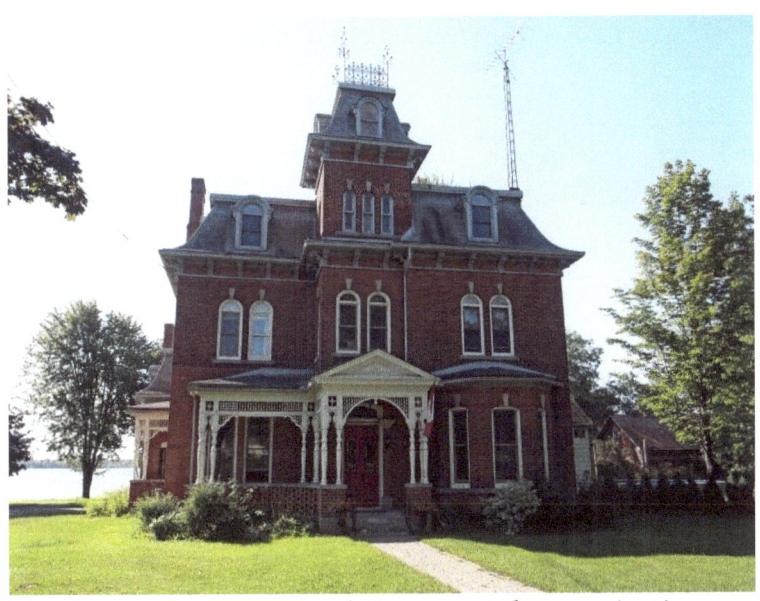

31 Lakeshore Drive – Second Empire style – projecting central tower, concave mansard roof, dormers; has eighteen stained glass windows, each with a different color scheme

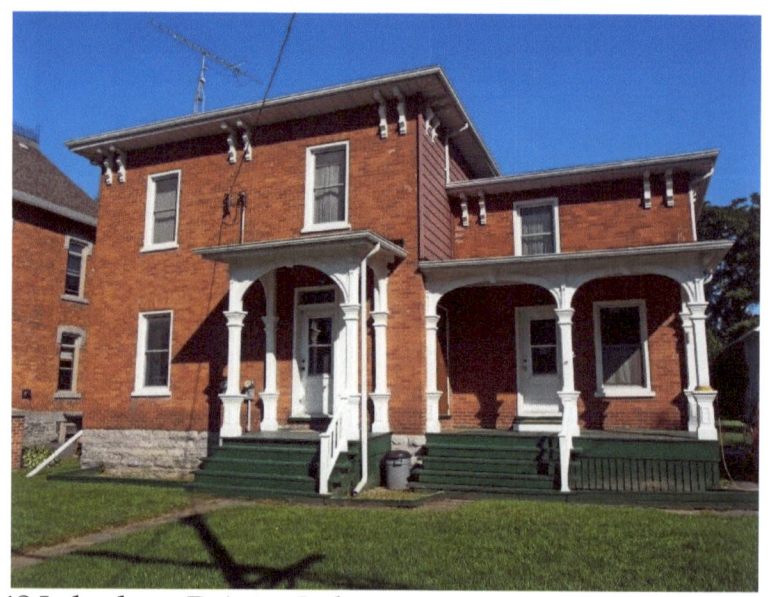

48 Lakeshore Drive – Italianate, paired cornice brackets, decorative porch and verandah supports; transom

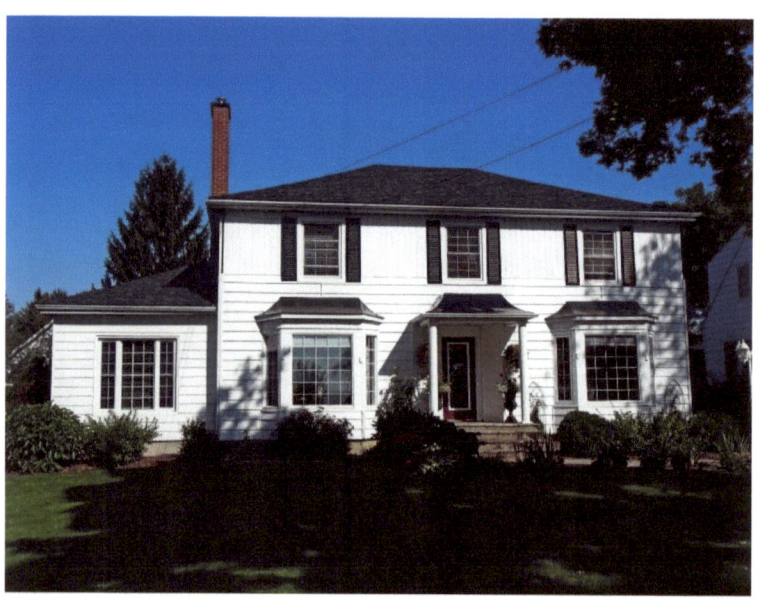

Lakeshore Drive – Georgian style – hipped roof, balanced façade, bay windows

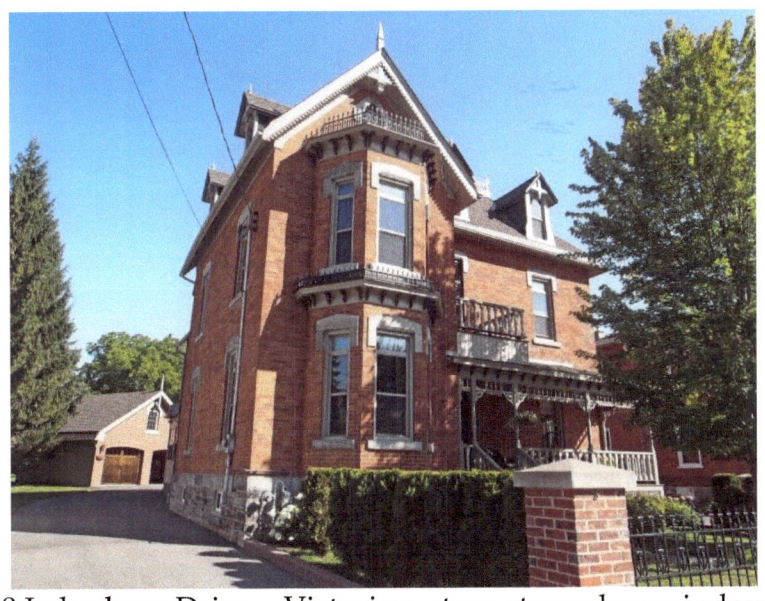

50 Lakeshore Drive – Victorian – two-storey bay windows with iron cresting above, widow's walk balcony on rooftop with iron cresting, dormers with finials; verandah with ornate capital detailing on the support posts with spindles under the cornice

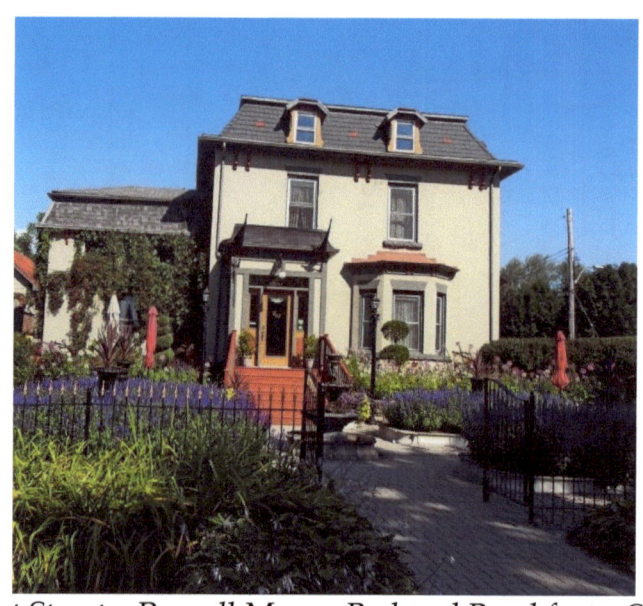

36 First Street – Russell Manor Bed and Breakfast – Second Empire style, mansard roof, cornice brackets, patterned slate roof, bay window

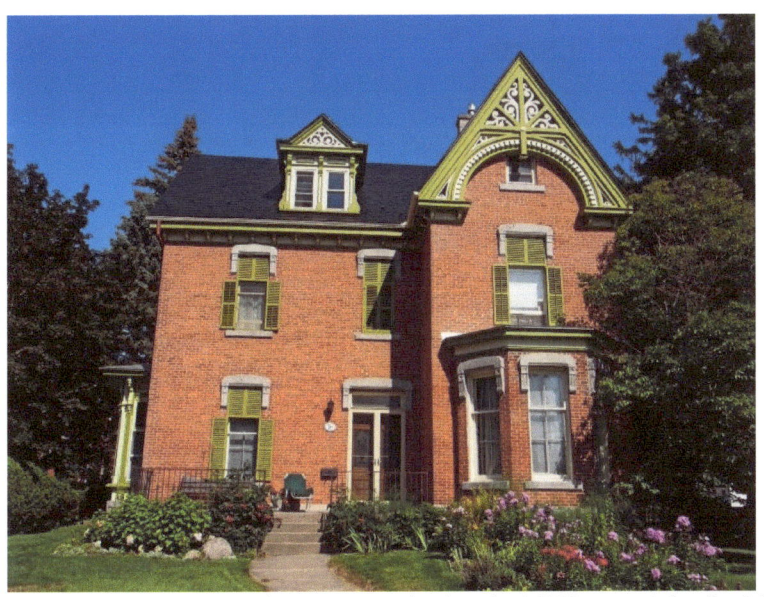

16 First Street – Gothic Revival - built 1870s – wide, bold bargeboards, central pinnacle suspended beneath the peak ending in a knob-like pendant above the third floor window; intricate cut-out patterns adorning the gable ends

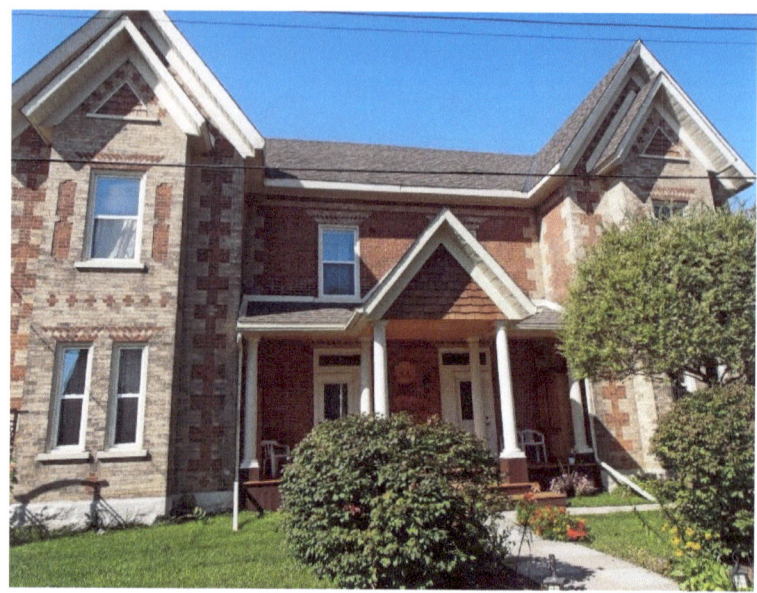

24 High Street – Gothic Revival style – symmetrical organization, steeply pitched roof gables, tall twin window bays; dichromatic brickwork; transom windows

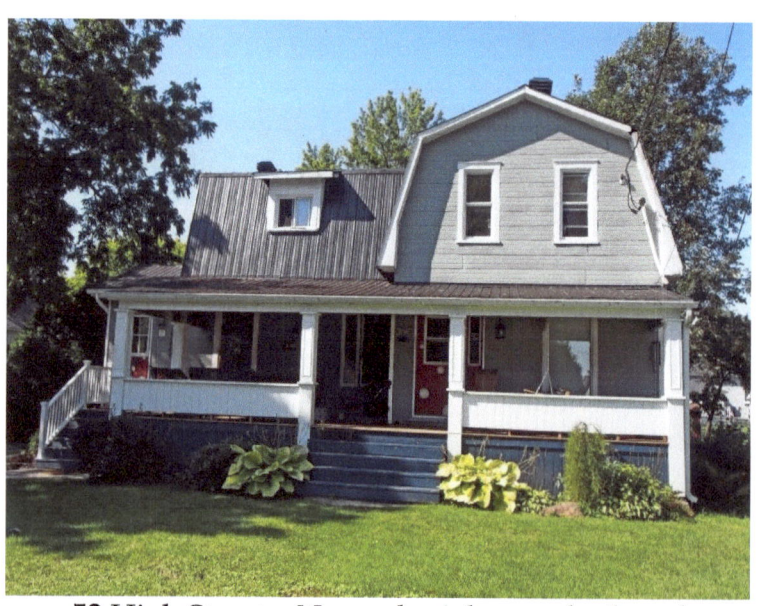

52 High Street – Neo-colonial – gambrel roof

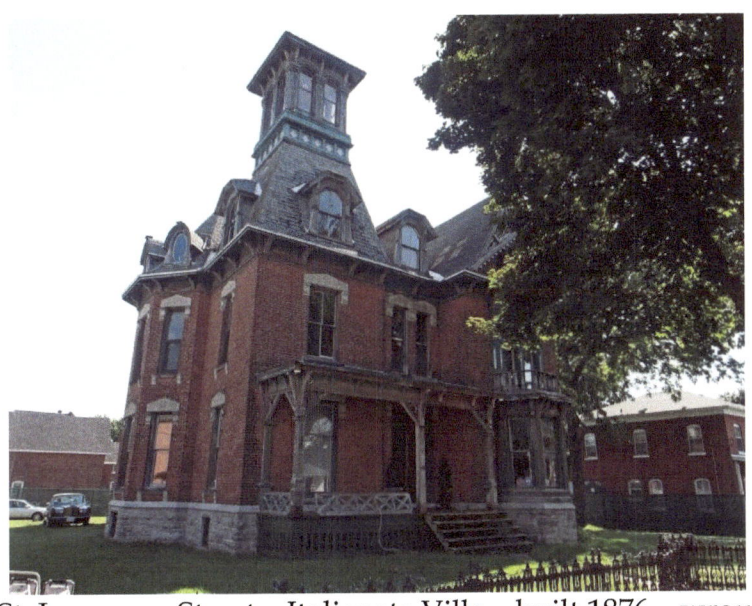

19 St. Lawrence Street – Italianate Villa – built 1876 – wrought iron fence; corner tower with its tall, four-sided lantern contains four pairs of Italianate round headed windows; classic Italianate porch and front door

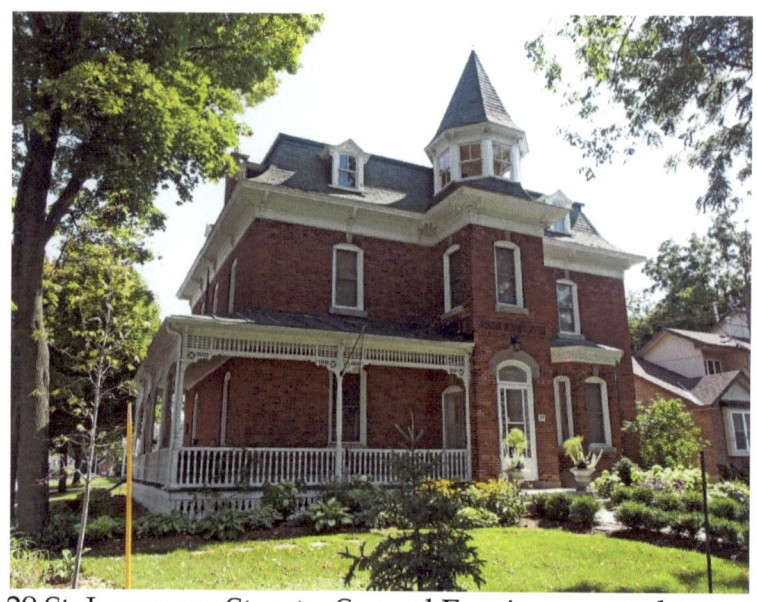

29 St. Lawrence Street – Second Empire – central tower directly above the front door topped with a belvedere; mansard roof with dormers

Brockville, Ontario – My Top 12 Picks

Brockville, formerly Elizabethtown, is a city in Eastern Ontario in the Thousand Islands region located on the north shore of the Saint Lawrence River opposite Morristown, New York. It is about halfway between Cornwall to the east and Kingston to the west. It is one of Ontario's oldest European-Canadian communities and is named after the British General Sir Isaac Brock.

This area of Ontario was first settled by English speaking people in 1785, when thousands of American refugees arrived from the American colonies after the American Revolutionary War. They were later called United Empire Loyalists because of their allegiance to King George III. The struggle between Britain and the 13 American colonies occurred in the years 1776 to 1783, and divided loyalties among the people. During the 6-year war, which ended with the capitulation of the British in 1782, many colonists who remained loyal to the crown were subject to harsh reprisals and unfair dispossession of their property by their countrymen. Many Loyalists chose to flee north to the British colony of Quebec. Great Britain opened the western region of Canada (known as Upper Canada and now Ontario), purchasing land from First Nations to allocate to the Loyalists in compensation for their losses, and helping them with some supplies as they founded new settlements. In 1785 the first Loyalist to take up land in Brockville was William Buell Senior, an ensign disbanded from the King's Rangers from the State of New York.

In the 19th century the town developed as a local center of industry, including shipbuilding, saddleries, tanneries, tinsmiths, a foundry, a brewery, and several hotels.

In 1855, Brockville was chosen as a divisional point of the new Grand Trunk Railway between Montreal and Toronto. At the same time, the north-south line of the Brockville and Ottawa Railway was built to join the timber trade of the Ottawa Valley with the St. Lawrence River ship route. A well-engineered tunnel for this railway was dug and blasted underneath the middle of Brockville. The Brockville Tunnel was the first railway tunnel in Canada.

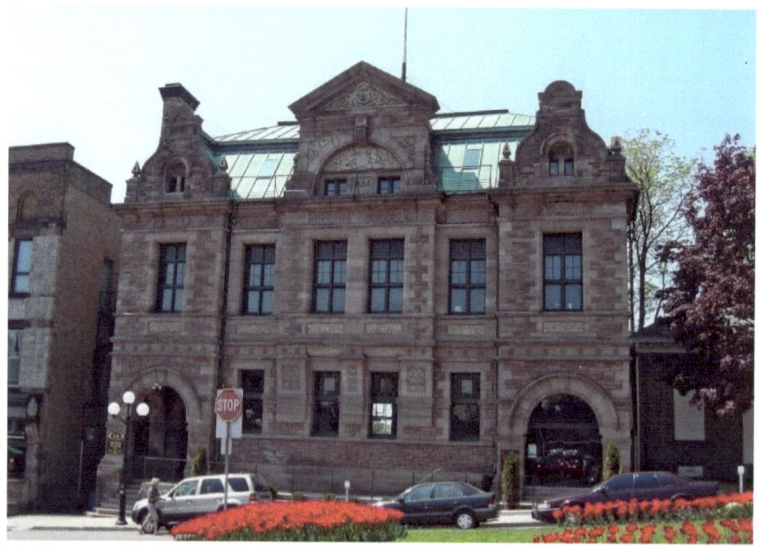

12-14 Court House Avenue – Thomas Fuller Building – former Post Office – 1883-85 - A stone post office, blending Flemish, Queen Anne and Classical elements; a good example of the post offices erected by the Department of Public Works in smaller urban centers during Thomas Fuller's term as Chief Dominion Architect.

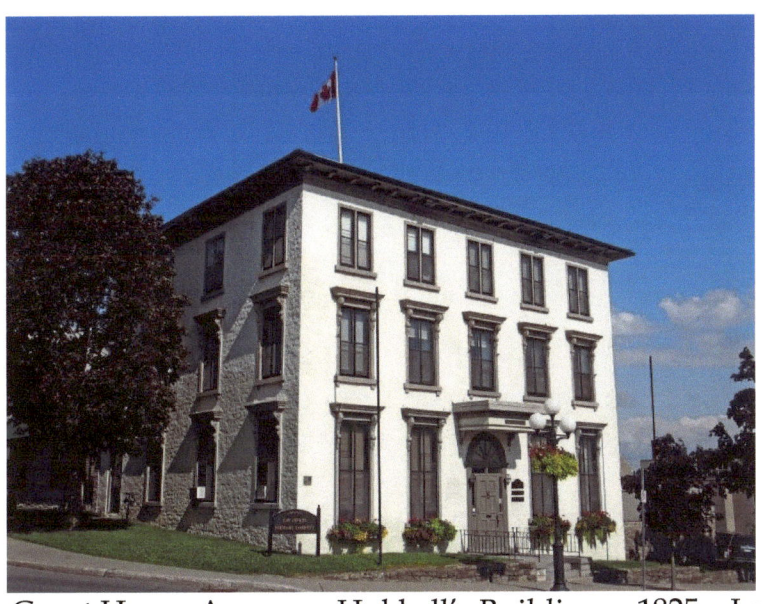

21 Court House Avenue – Hubbell's Building c. 1825 – Law Offices Stewart Corbett – window hoods with cornice brackets, semi-circular transom and sidelights

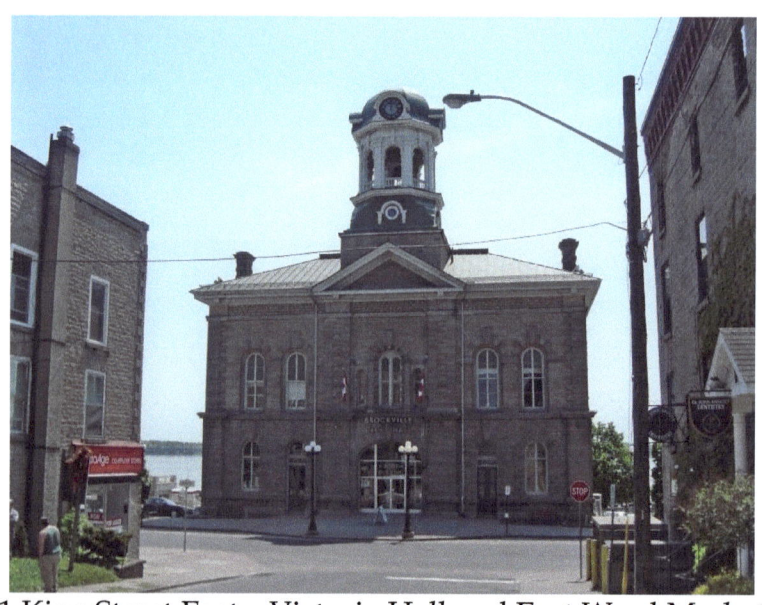

1 King Street East – Victoria Hall and East Ward Market Building – 1863 – designed to show off the success and taste of Brockville s inhabitants – built as a combination concert hall, office space and indoor market house – stone building, intricate detailing, and beautiful clock tower

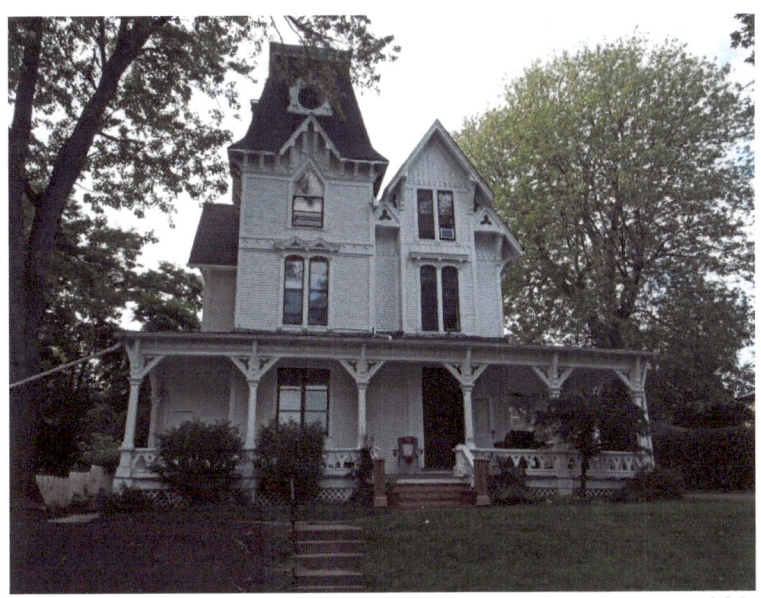

112 King Street East – Alexander Allan House – c. 1880 - Victorian Villa in the Stick Style – irregular in shape, three bays, clapboard sided, four stories, tower, mansard roof, iron cresting, cornice brackets, window hoods, trefoil designs on house and veranda supports

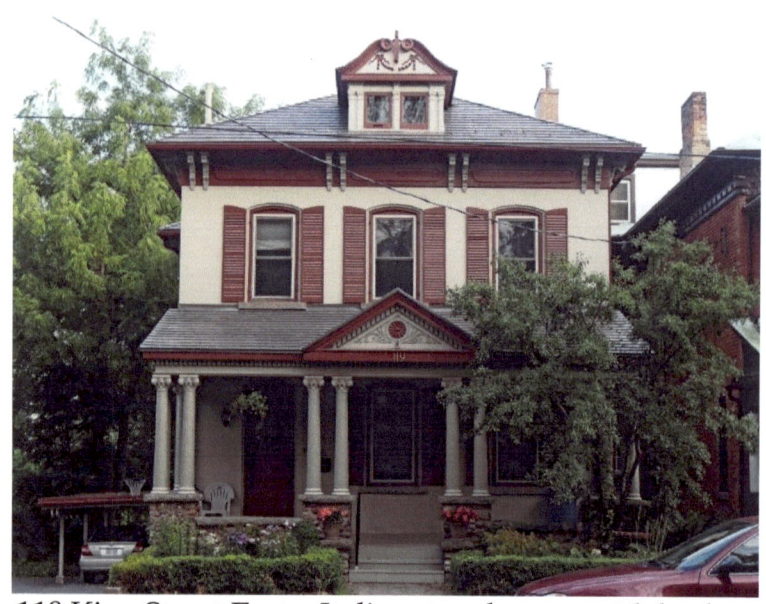

119 King Street East – Italianate - dormer with broken pediment and decorated tympanum; hipped roof; paired cornice brackets; composite pillars supporting veranda with pediment and decorative tympanum

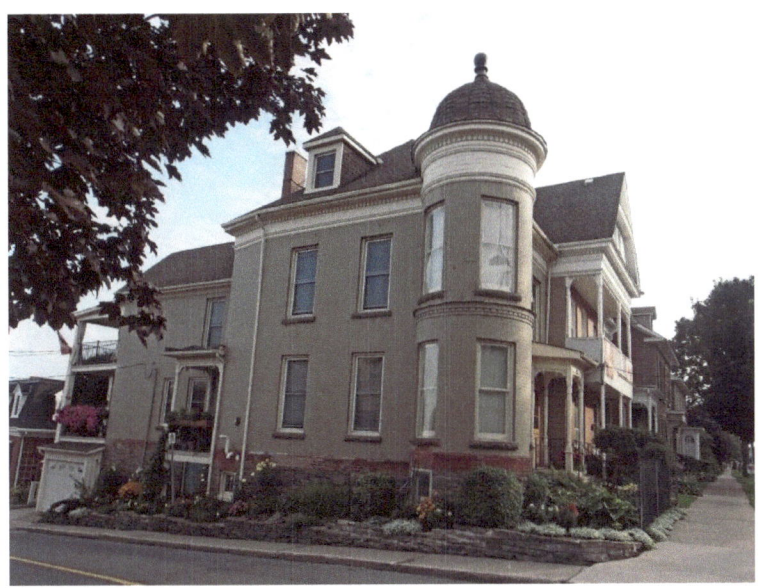

135 King Street East – Brace Terrace (131-135) – c. 1896 - two storey circular tower; dormer, dentil molding; wood turned porch supports

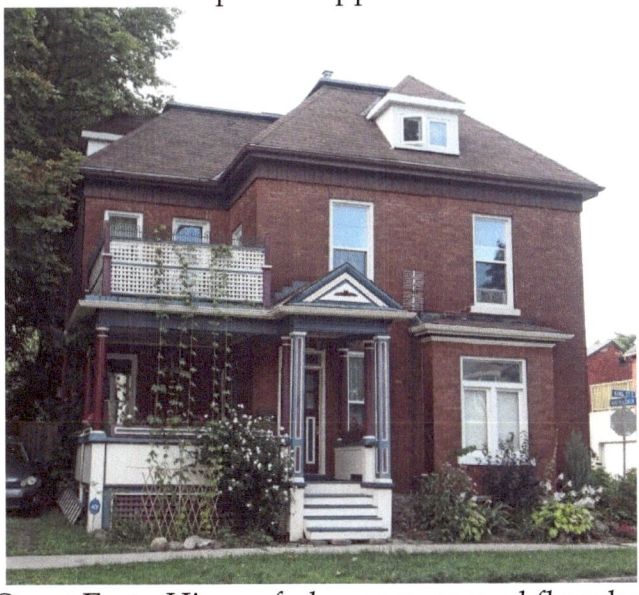

King Street East - Hip roof, dormers, second floor balcony, pediment above verandah supported by rectangular and circular pillars, rectangular bay window

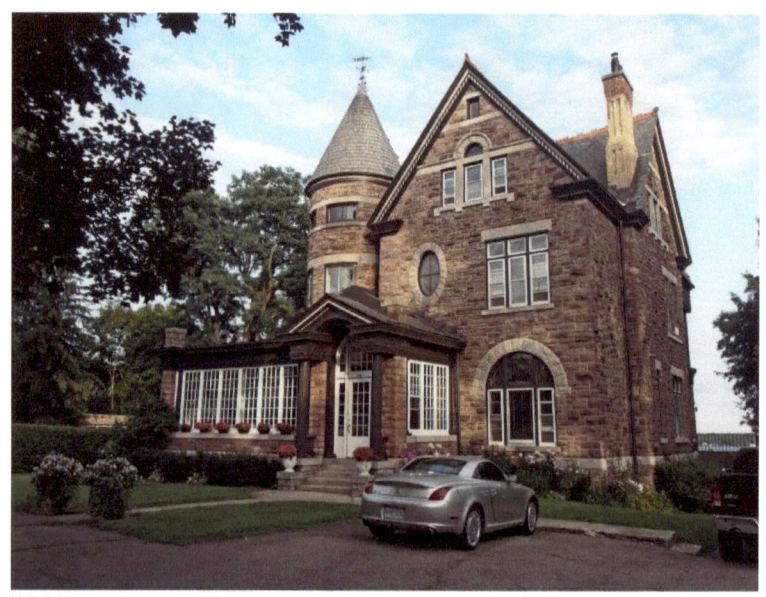

165 King Street East – Romanesque style, tower, Palladian window in gable with cornice return, large decorative chimney, round window arch, circular window, open pediment, enclosed veranda

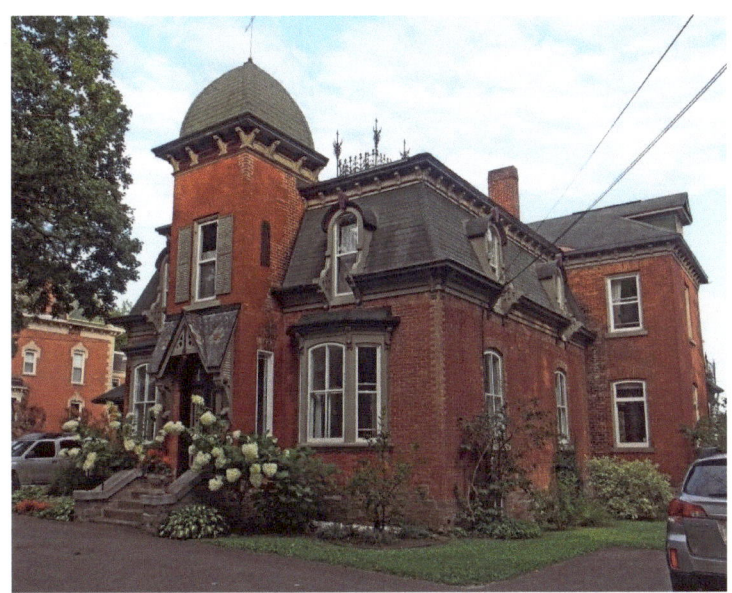

181 King Street East – Gill House – 1878 additions of roof and wings - Second Empire style, mansard roof, dormers, window hoods with keystones, iron cresting around rooftop balcony, central tower, bay windows

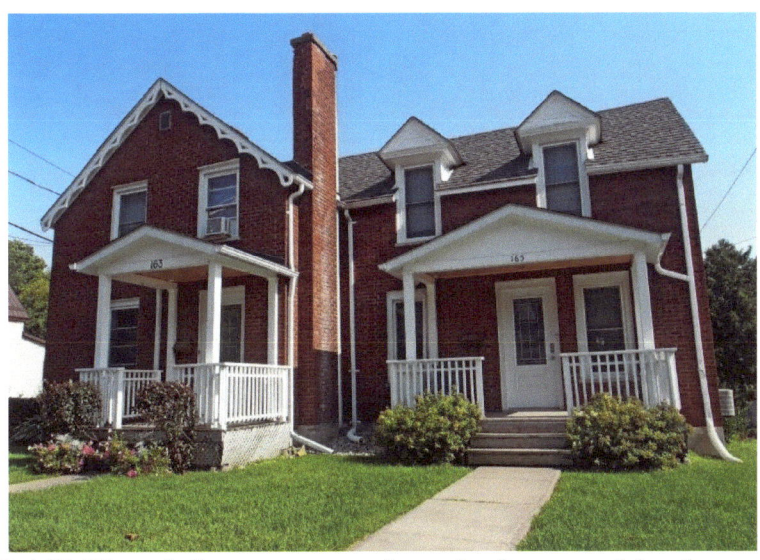

163-165 Church Street – verge board trim on gable, dormers, pediments

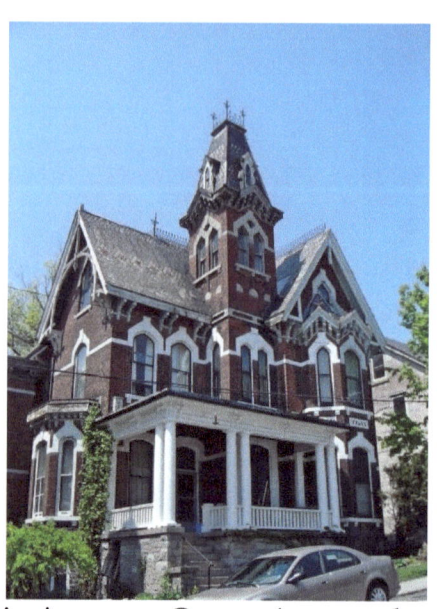

12 Victoria Avenue - Queen Anne style – tower, iron cresting; stone keystones and banding; verge board trim, finials; bay windows; veranda with Doric columns

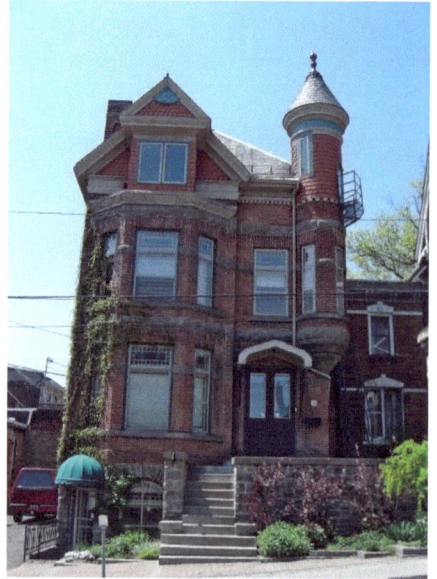

10 Victoria Avenue - Queen Anne style – turret with stone lintels, corbelling and banding; 2-storey bay windows

Merrickville, Ontario – My Top 16 Picks

The United Empire Loyalists were the first non-aboriginal people to settle in the Merrickville area. Beginning in 1783, they were forced to leave the United States after the British defeat in the American War of Independence. Most of these settlers were farmers of Welsh, German, Dutch, Scottish and Irish descent. By settling along the Rideau River, they had access to rich soil, a source of fresh water, and a communication lifeline as the river could keep them connected to each other and to other communities along its banks. In 1793, William Merrick acquired a saw mill from Roger Stevens at the "Great Falls" on the Rideau River (there was a drop of fourteen feet in the river), and then began building new mills which formed the nucleus of Merricks Mills.

As industry grew, farms provided the mills with resources to process. Lumber, corn, oats, wheat, hides, and wool kept the mills running and ensured the region's growing prosperity. Transporting agricultural goods and raw materials such as pig iron became even easier with the construction of the Rideau Canal. From the 1850s to the 1890s, Merrickville was a very important manufacturing center along the Rideau corridor.

Wheels and tools to cut, saw, seed, cultivate, harvest and store agricultural crops were very important. In the 1850s Merrickville leached wood ashes and evaporated the liquid to make potash; they produced twenty barrels, each weighing five hundred pounds, in a year. Potash was used in fertilizers, soaps and other manufactured goods. A cooperage in Merrickville was established in 1845; coopers produced butter churns, tubs, and barrels (for flour, salt pork, etc.). Several brickyards offered an alternative to wood and stone for building materials. Several tanneries were located here; they produced leather from animal skins.

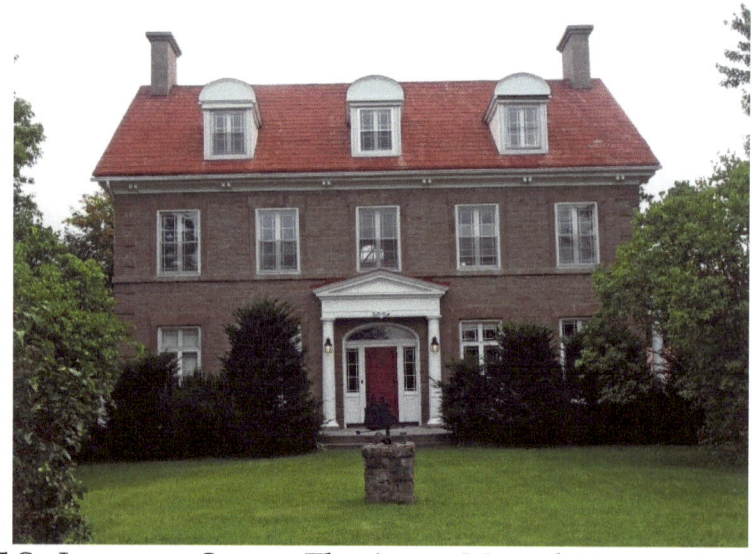

905 St. Lawrence Street - The Aaron Merrick House – built in 1844 of local stone with refined stone window surrounds and oversized stone quoins for the son of the founder of Merrick's Mills – Georgian style with distinct Neo-classical detailing; dormers; semi-elliptical fanlight with sidelights frame a door found within a pedimented portico that is light and elegant

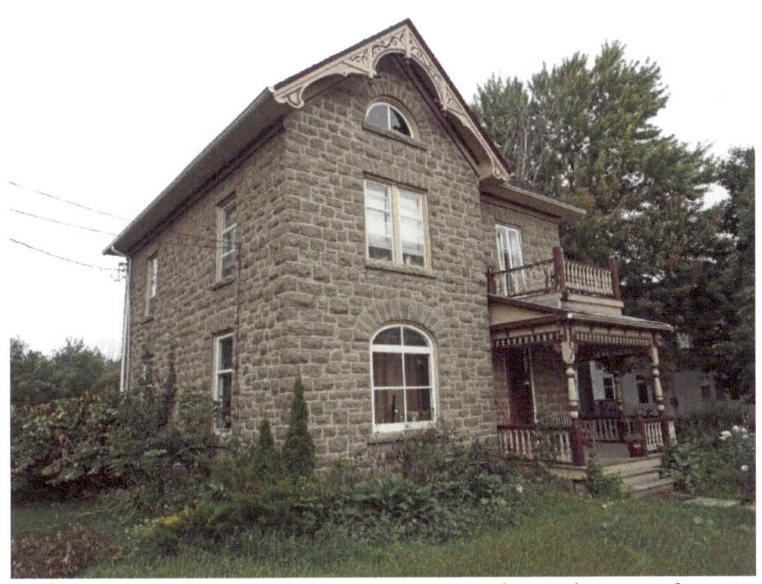

806 St. Lawrence Street – Gothic, verge board trim, decorative wood-turned spindles supporting second floor balcony

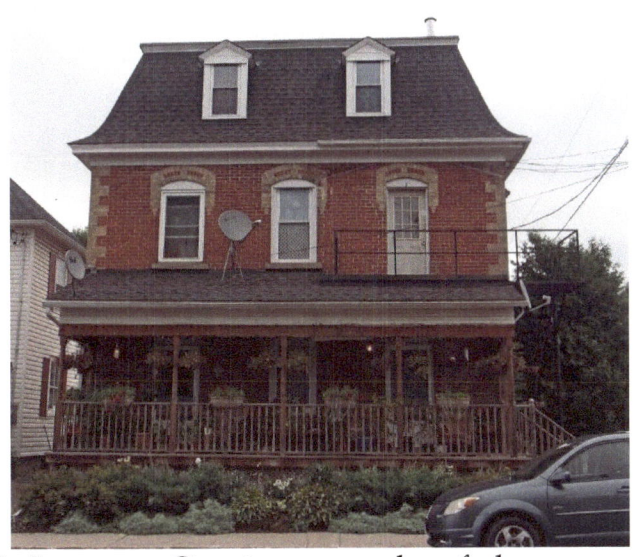

529 St. Lawrence Street – mansard roof, dormers, corner quoins, voussoirs

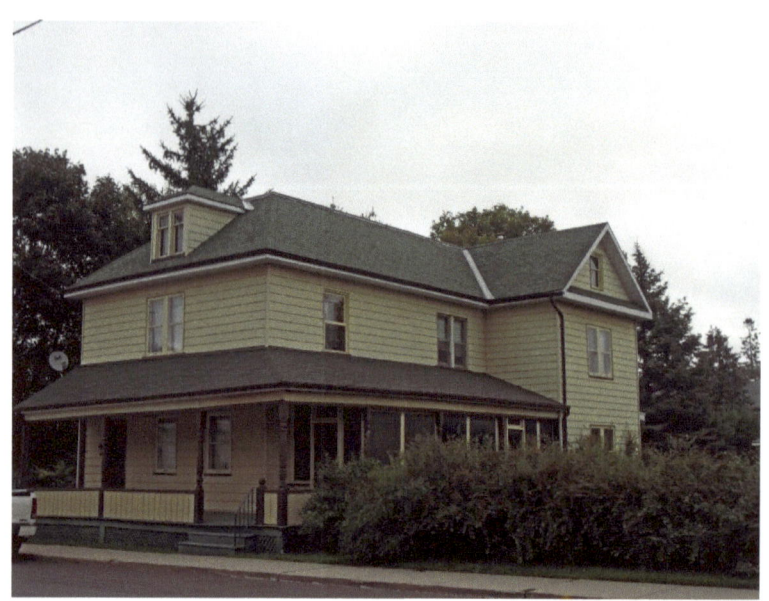

405 St. Lawrence Street – Dr. J. O. Walker House, c. 1870 – Family Physician (1912-1946) – hip roof, dormer

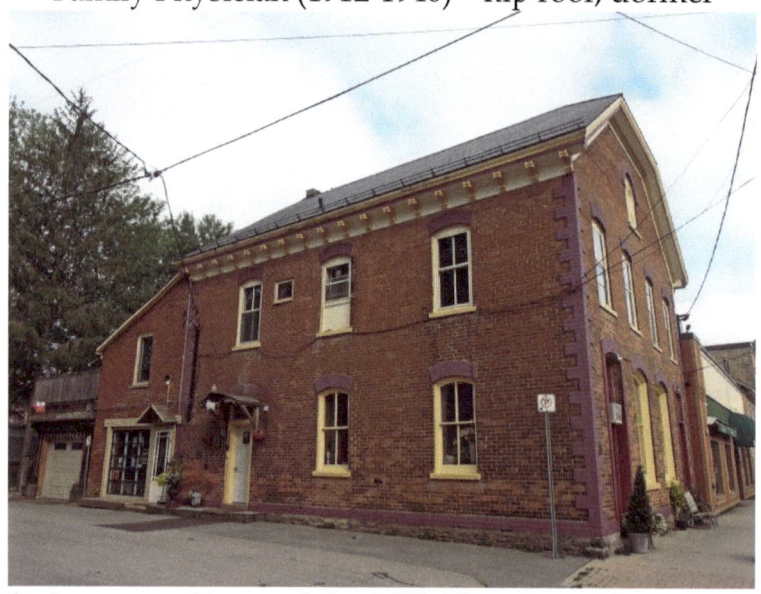

242 St. Lawrence Street – John Mills' Furniture Showroom and Funeral Home – c. 1868 – operated until the 1930s – corner quoins, cornice brackets

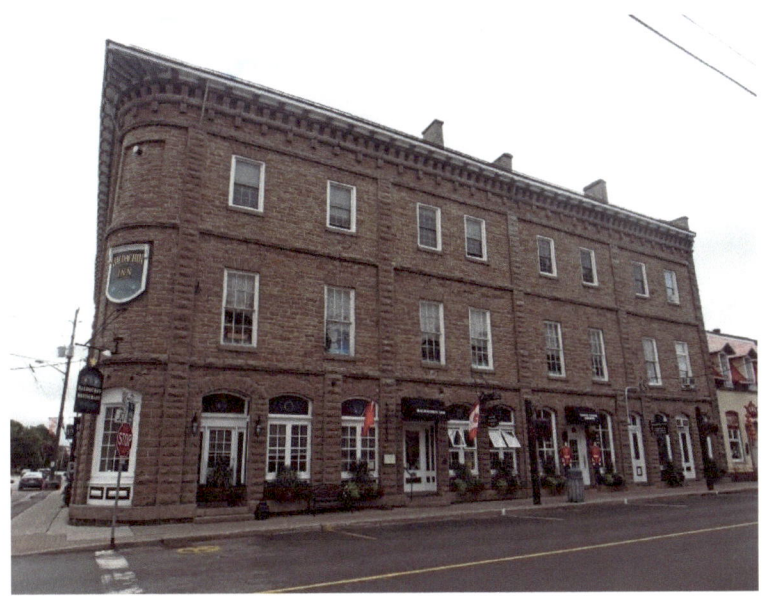

111 St. Lawrence Street – Jakes-McLean Block – c. 1862 – Baldachin Inn and Restaurant - dentil molding, pilasters, string courses, voussoirs

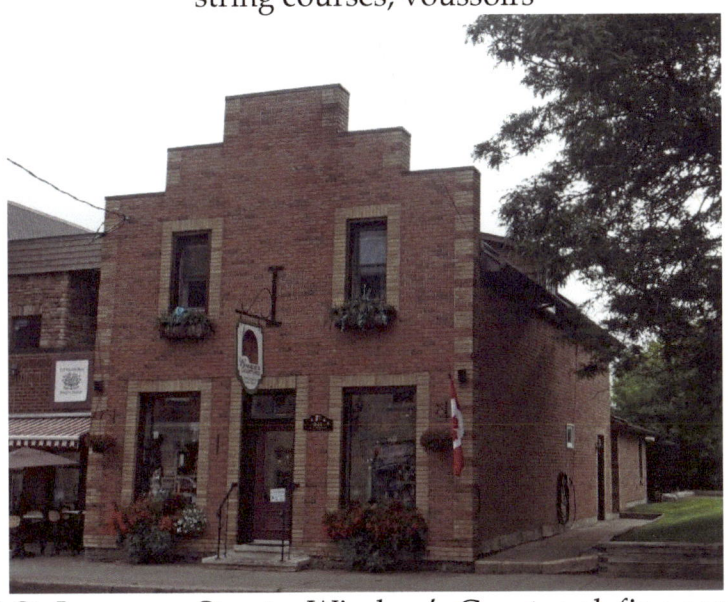

211 St. Lawrence Street – Windsor's Courtyard, fine garden and home décor – dichromatic brickwork, stepped parapet

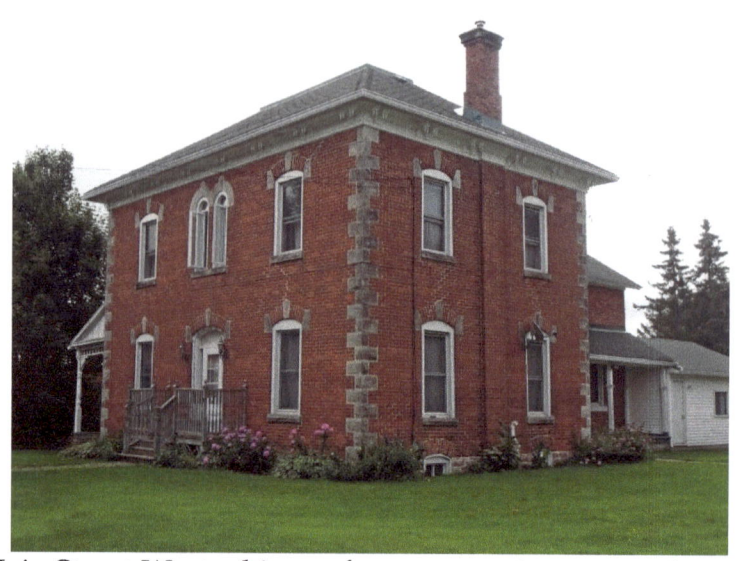

Main Street West – hip roof, corner quoins, voussoirs and keystones

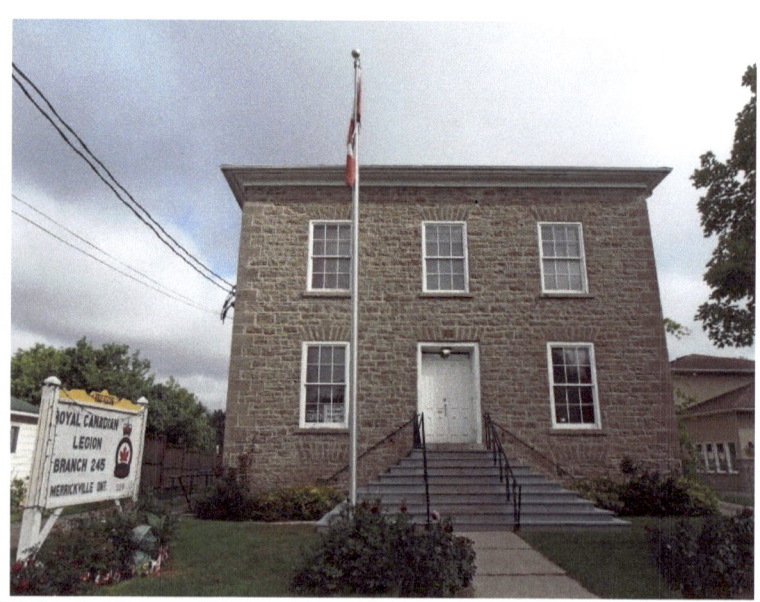

223 Main Street West - Royal Canadian Legion – old Town Hall - c. 1856 – stone, corner quoins

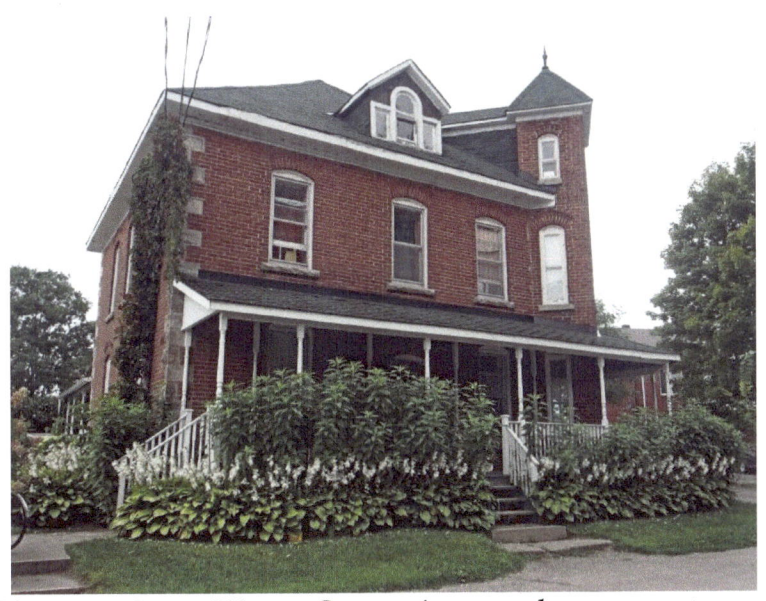

205 Main Street West – Queen Anne style – corner tower, dormer with Palladian window, turned veranda roof supports, open railing

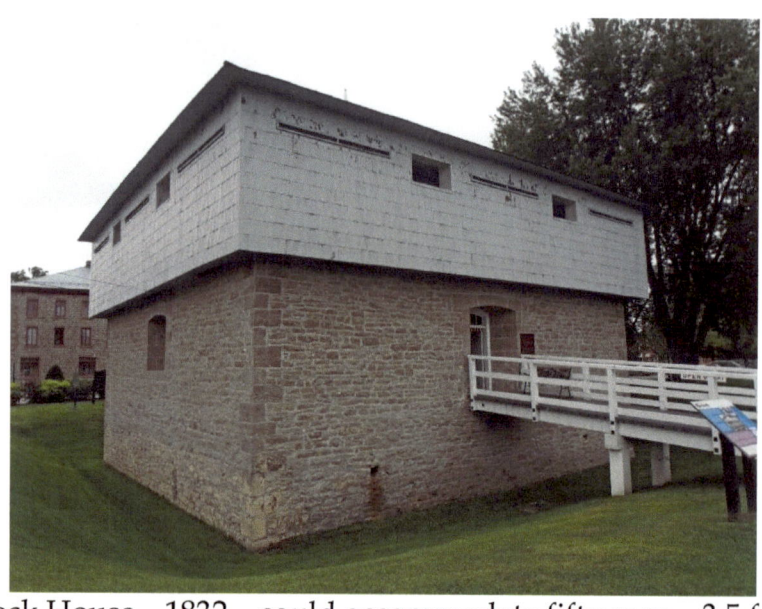

Block House – 1832 – could accommodate fifty men – 3.5 foot walls designed to withstand small cannon fire; pyramidal tin-sheathed roof to withstand torching; upper level overhang allowed for machicolated defense holes cut in the overhang to allow downward fire on an enemy; no military action here – served as lockmaster's quarters, a church, and a canal maintenance building – now a museum

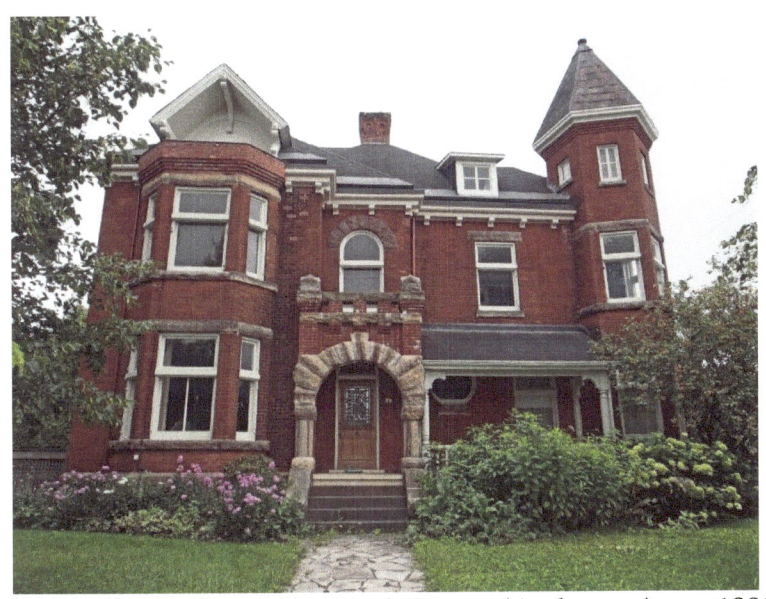

206 Main Street East – Percival House (Ardcaven) – c. 1890 – Richardsonian-Romanesque style – home of foundry-man Roger Percival – heavy stone arch around door, decorative chimney, two-storey bay window topped with open pediment, dormer, tower, stone courses

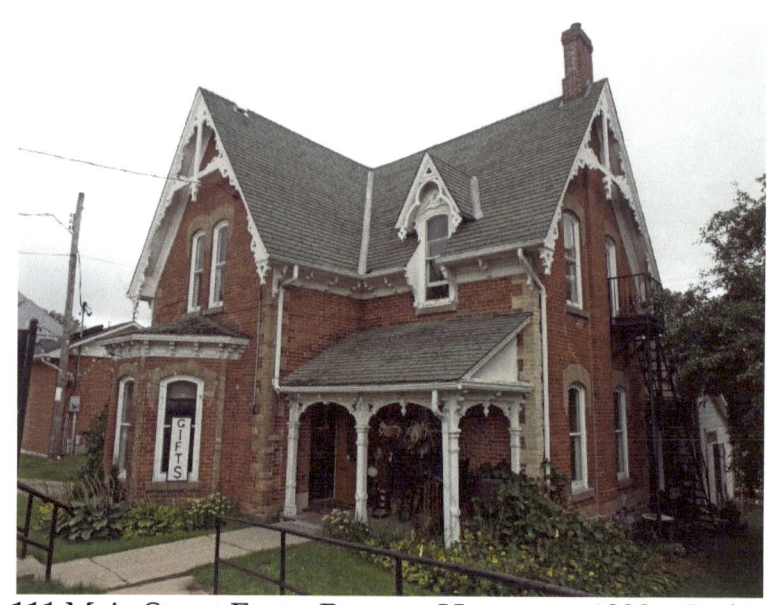

111 Main Street East – Pearson House – c. 1890 - Gothic Revival – former location of the Merrickville Public Library - verge board trim with finials on gables, dormer, bay window; veranda roof supports with ornate capital detailing

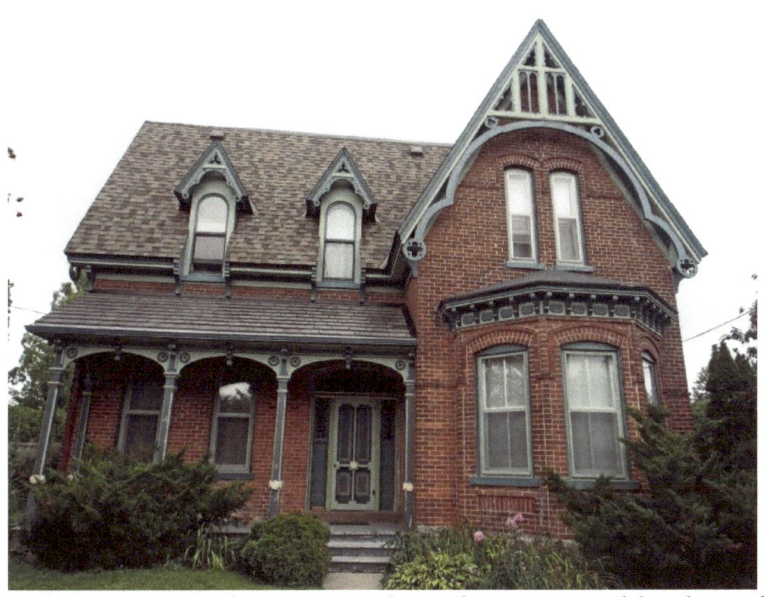

Church Street – Gothic – verge board trim on gable above bay window, dormers, pillars with decorative capitals

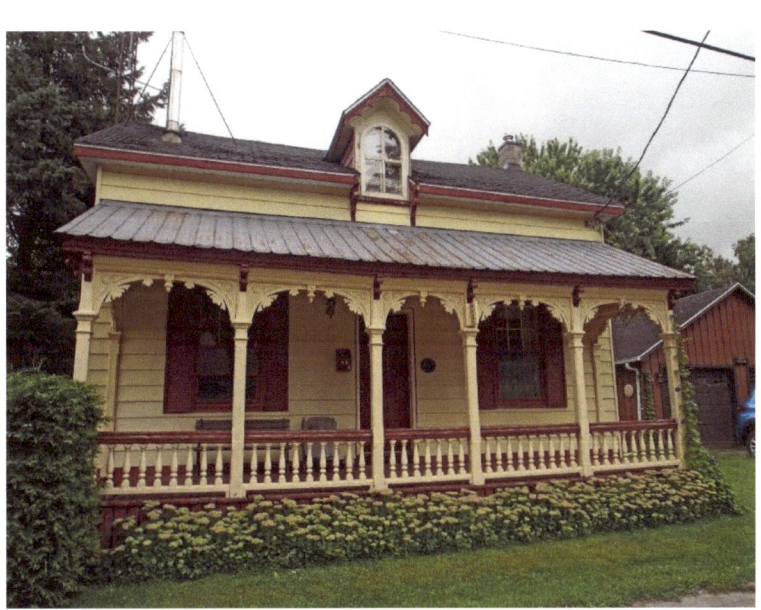

405 Elgin Street - decorative capitals on veranda supports, open spindle railing; dormer in attic

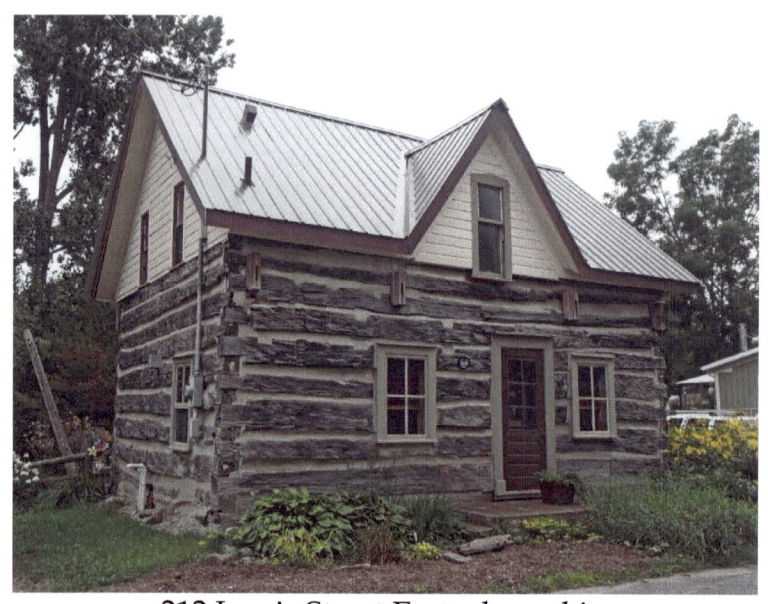

212 Lewis Street East – log cabin

Smiths Falls, Ontario – My Top 8 Picks

Smiths Falls is a town in Eastern Ontario located fourteen miles east of Perth. The Rideau Canal waterway passes through the town, with four separate locks in three locations and a combined lift of over fifteen metres (fifty feet). The city is named after Thomas Smyth, a United Empire Loyalist who in 1786 was granted 400 acres here. In 1846, there were fifty dwellings, two grist mills (one with four run of stones), two sawmills, one carding and fulling mill, seven stores, six groceries, one axe factory, six blacksmiths, two wheelwrights, one cabinet maker, one chair-maker, three carpenters, one gunsmith, eleven shoemakers, seven tailors, one tinsmith and two taverns.

At the time of construction of the Rideau Canal a small settlement had been established around a mill operated by Abel Russell Ward, who had bought Smyth's land. Colonel By ordered the removal of Ward's mill to make way for the canal. The disruption of industry caused by the building of the canal was only temporary, and Smiths Falls grew rapidly following construction.

The Rideau Canal area is home to a variety of ecosystems. The land along the Rideau that was once logged is now home to deep-rooted deciduous and coniferous forests that have been maturing for over one hundred years. Where the landscape flattens, there are cedar/hardwood swamps, bogs and cattail marshes which support the healthy wildlife population.

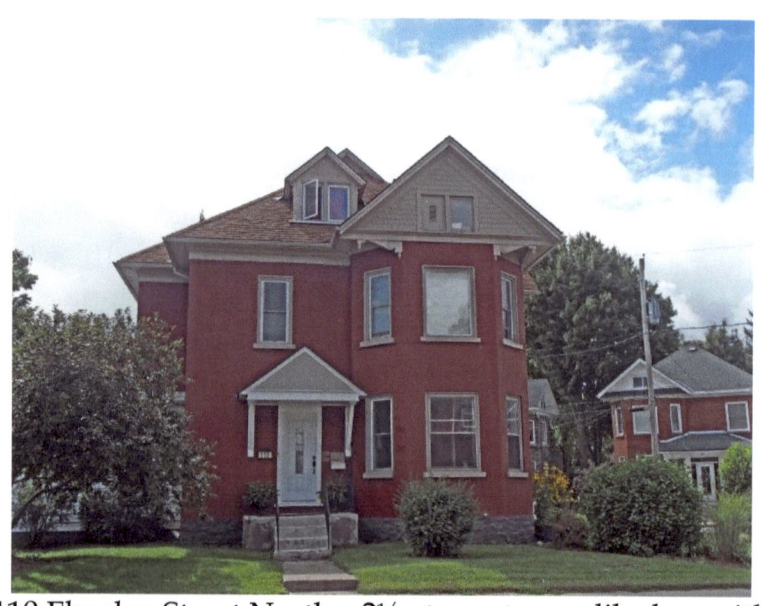

110 Elmsley Street North – 2½-storey tower-like bay with pediment and fretwork; dormer

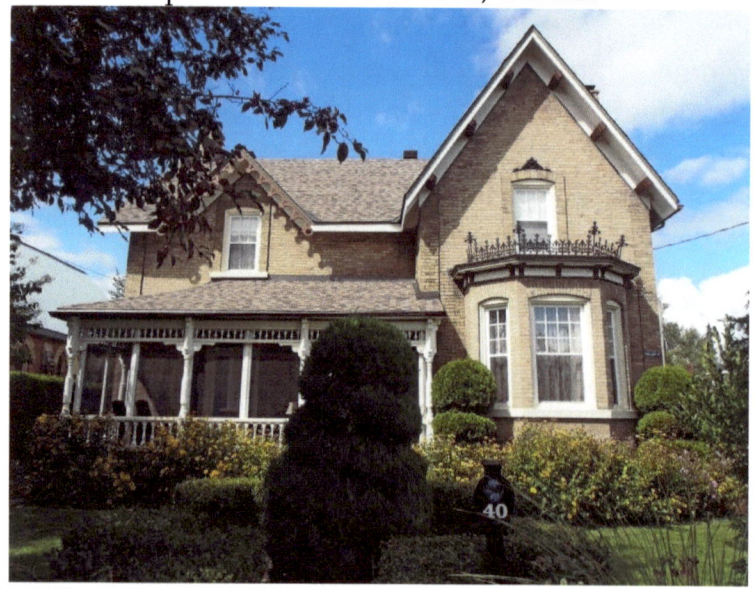

40 William Street – Victorian – iron cresting around balcony above bay window; turned veranda roof supports with decorative capitals and spindles

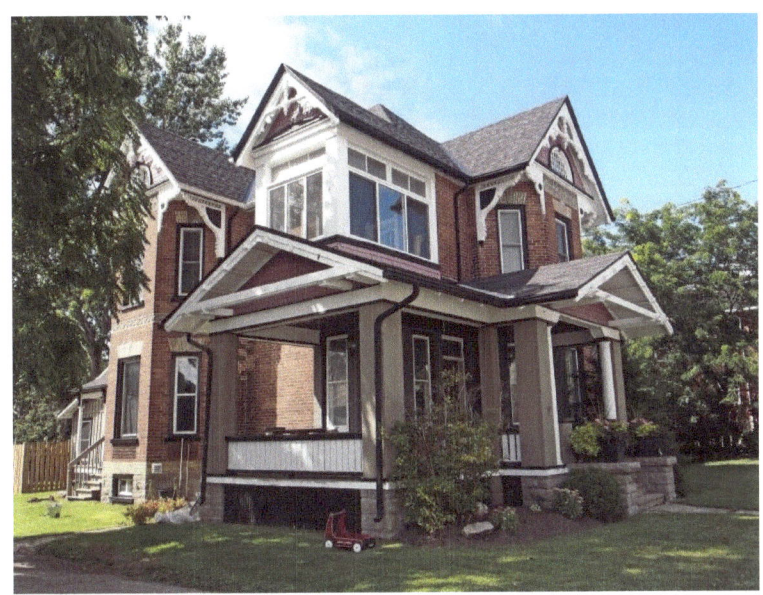

16 Maple Avenue – Victorian Cottage style – c. late 1890s – double bay windows, high gables decorated with detailed wood trim and finials, fretwork, voussoirs and keystones, dichromatic brickwork and banding; upper exterior porch; elegant entrance

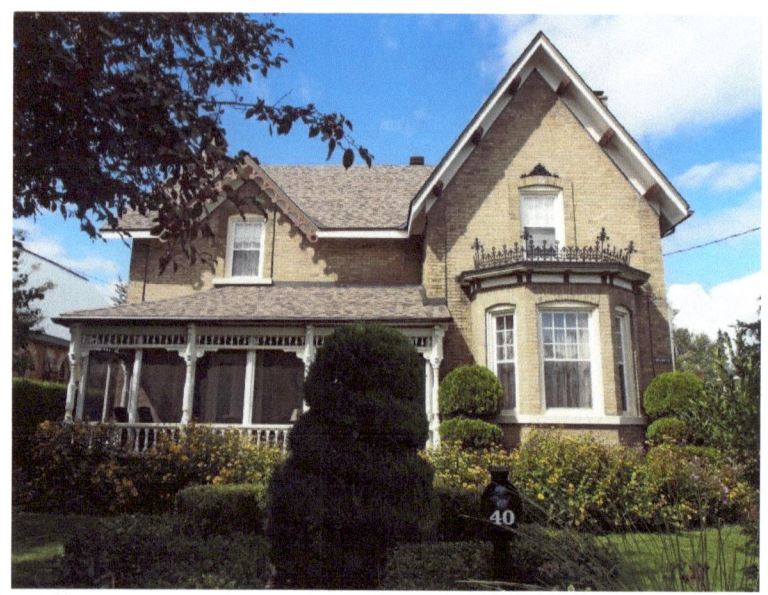

40 William Street – Victorian – iron cresting around balcony above bay window; turned veranda roof supports with decorative capitals and spindles

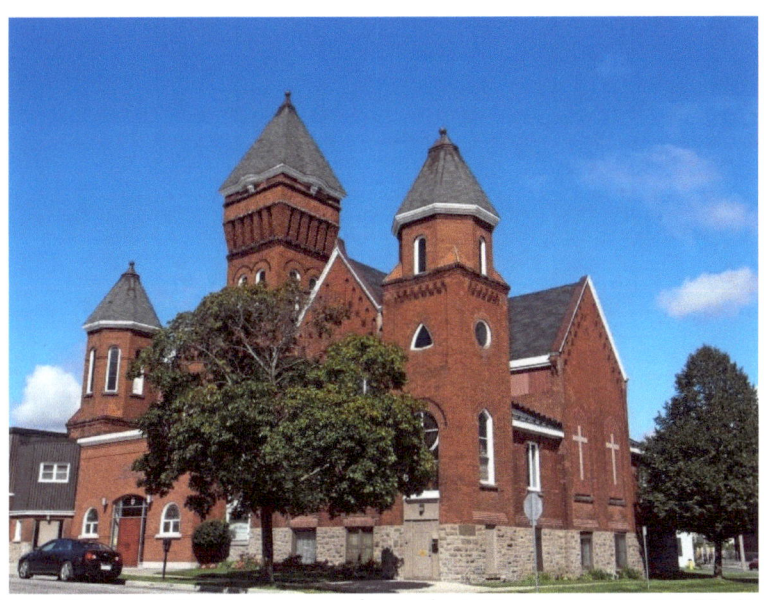

Russell Street East corner of Market Street – Trinity United Church – 1886 – Queen Anne style – three non-symmetrical towers, various shaped windows, rose window, bevelled dentil molding

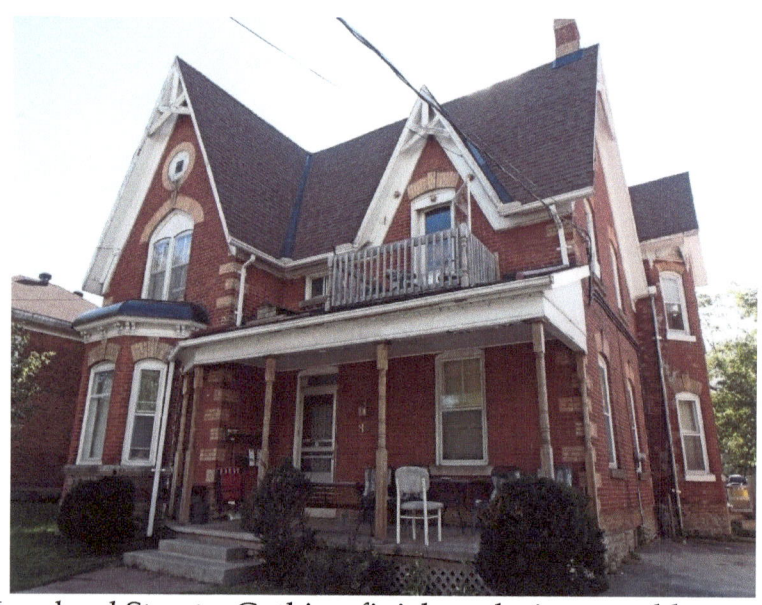

84 Lombard Street – Gothic – finials and trim on gables, corner quoins, voussoirs with keystones, second floor balcony; bay window with cornice brackets; turned spindle roof supports for veranda

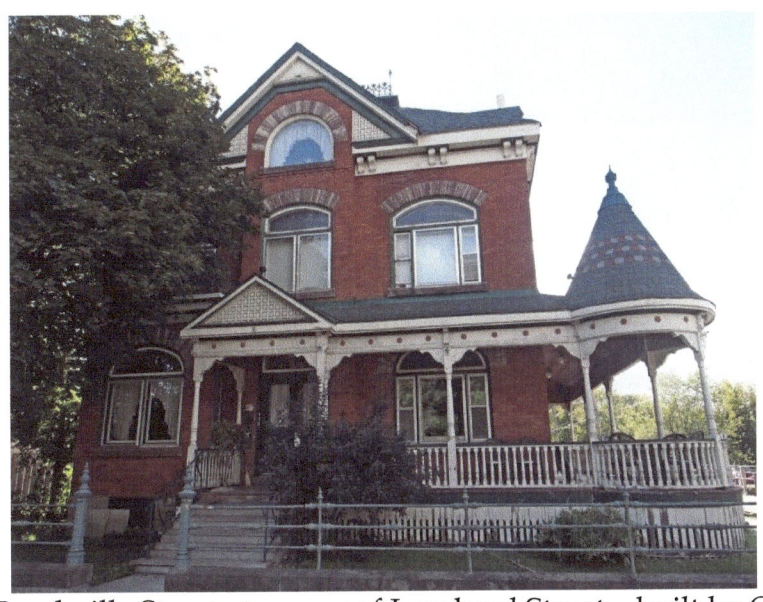

78 Brockville Street at corner of Lombard Street – built by Ogle Carss, an early mayor of the town – 1895 – Queen Anne Revival style – irregular outline, broad gables, multi-sloped roofs, a belvedere, a tower, ornamental cast iron railings on the roof; long, graceful wraparound verandah; stone voussoirs over semi-circular windows with transoms

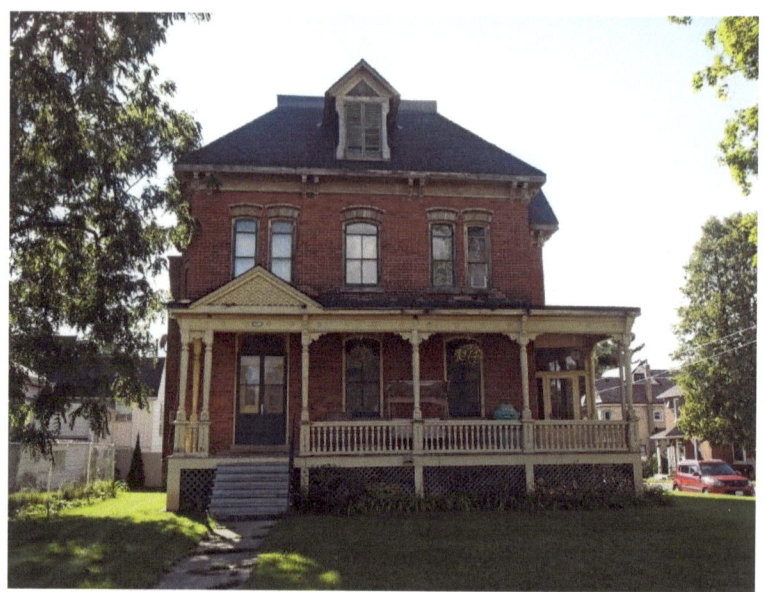

102 Brockville Street – Italianate - steeply pitched hip roof with dormer; cornice brackets, voussoirs; turned veranda roof supports with decorative capitals, open railing; pediment

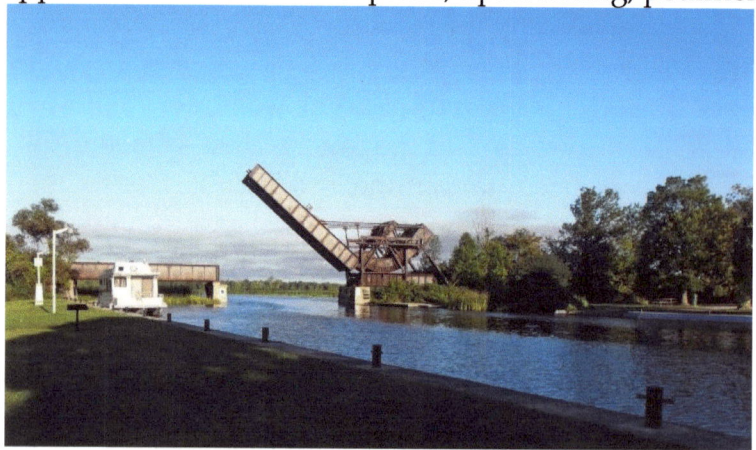

Bascule Bridge – located west of the Detached Locks – a rolling-lift railway bridge built in 1914, now in a permanently raised position – it works like a seesaw – on one end a hinged counter weight drops causing the other end to rise – it was the solution to the point where the railway and canal intersected

Portland and Newboro, Ontario – My Top 12 Picks

Portland is a community located in Eastern Ontario within the township of Rideau Lakes in the United Counties of Leeds and Grenville. It is north of Kingston and situated on Big Rideau Lake.

Portland was first settled in the early nineteenth century as one of the first settlements along the Rideau Waterway. With the completion of the Rideau Canal Waterway in 1832, steamboats and barges carried raw materials such as cordwood, maple syrup, potash, cheese, tanned hides and salt beef. Portland became a thriving village of trade with Kingston, Montreal and Ottawa.

The village of Portland took its name in 1843 from William Cavendish-Bentinck, 3rd Duke of Portland, a British Whig and Tory statesman, Chancellor of the University of Oxford, and served as Prime Minister of Great Britain in 1783 and Prime Minister of the United Kingdom from 1807 to 1809.

By the 1860s, the settlement had expanded considerably to require five hotels and, by the early twentieth century, cottages were built around the lake and the tourist trade began. Advances in rail and road travel and increasing tourism offset a decline in the role of agriculture in the economy of Portland. Tourism began to lead the economy and still does to this day.

An international speed skating tournament called Skate the Lake is held each winter on the Big Rideau Lake at Portland.

The settlement of the Newboro area was begun during the construction of the Rideau Canal in 1826-32. A major construction camp was located here at the Isthmus between the Rideau and Mud (Newboro) Lakes. In 1833, Benjamin Tett, owner of a nearby sawmill, opened a store and three years later a post office named Newborough was established. A small community including several stores developed as a trade center for the region's lumbering industry and agriculture. About 1850 a tannery was established and within ten years two iron mines were opened. The ore was exported via the Rideau to smelters in the United States. A foundry and a steam sawmill stimulated growth.

In 1888, a branch of the Brockville-Westport & S.S.M. Railroad came to Newboro. Trade and travel were now year-round. Produce of local farm and forest entered wider markets through Newboro's cannery and mills. From Newboro Station, local scholars went to and from high school in Athens and Brockville.

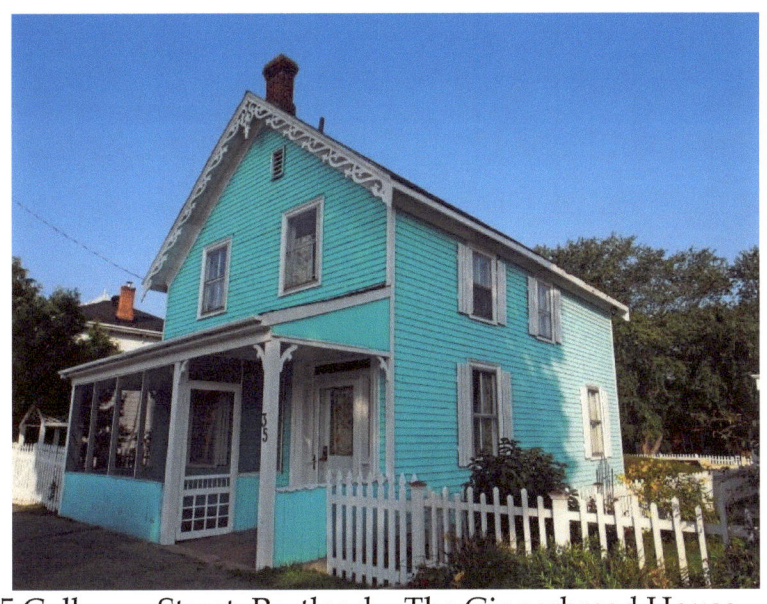

35 Colborne Street, Portland – The Gingerbread House – c. 1880s-1890s – Gothic Revival - gingerbread trim with finial on the front gable

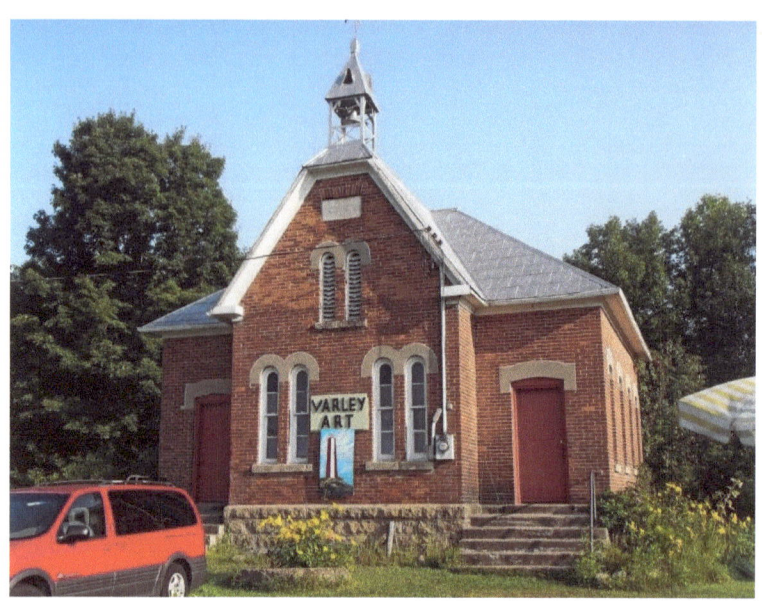

12 Newboro Road - Crosby Public School S.S. #2 – 1907 - now the site of Grace Varley's Art Gallery; separate entrances for boys and girls, tin roof, bell tower, voussoirs

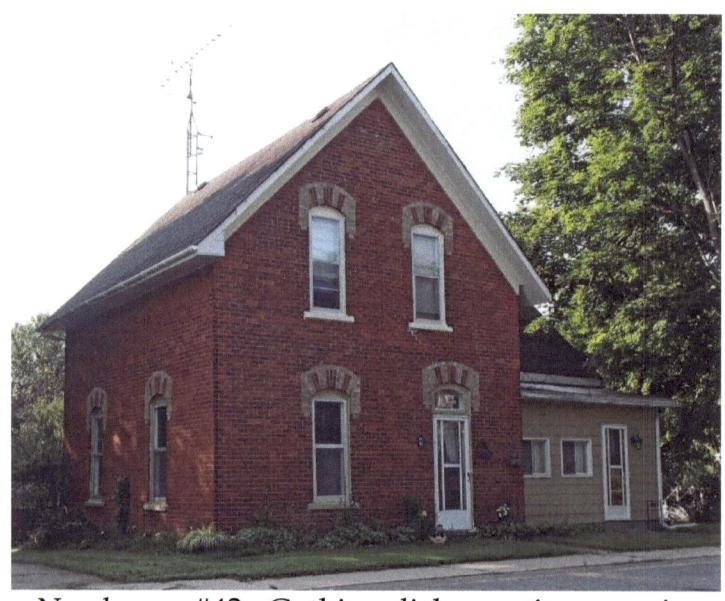

Newboro - #42 - Gothic – dichromatic voussoirs

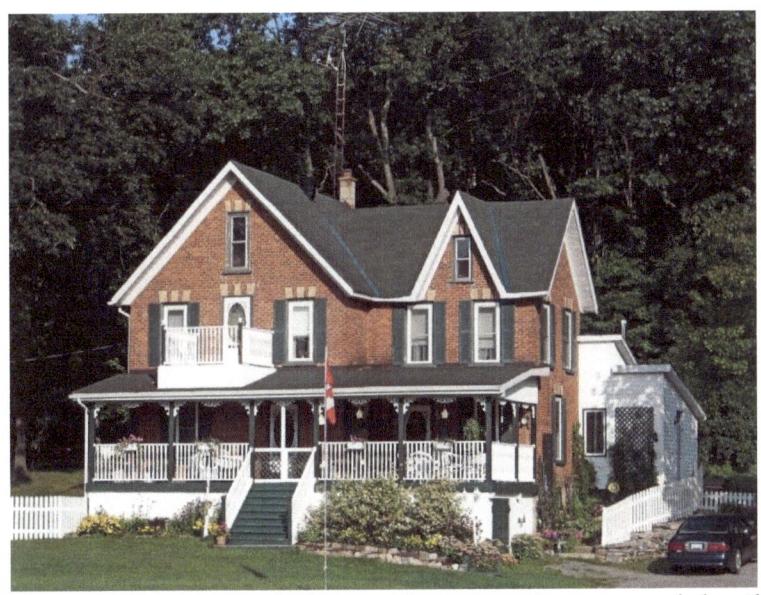

Newboro - Victorian - dichromatic voussoirs, verandah pillars with ornate capitals, open railing

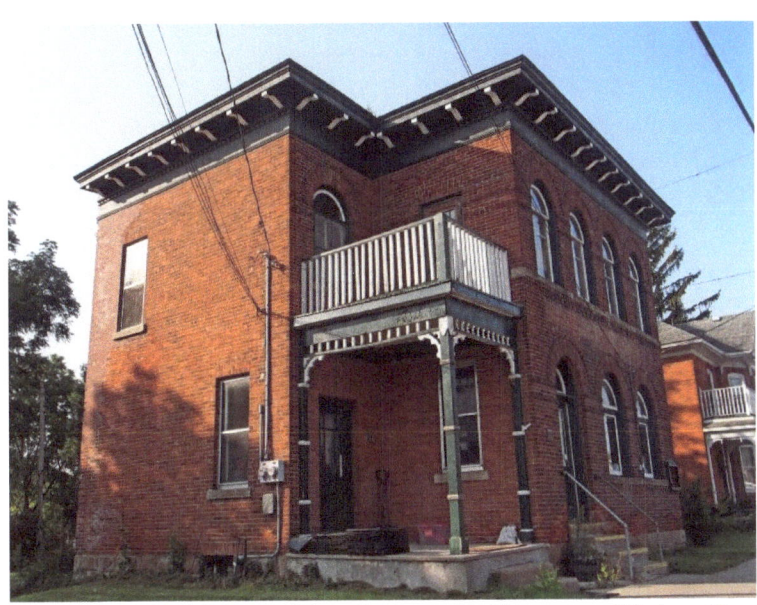

24 Drummond Street, Newboro – Italianate – Union Bank Building – cornice brackets, second floor balcony, voussoirs, string course

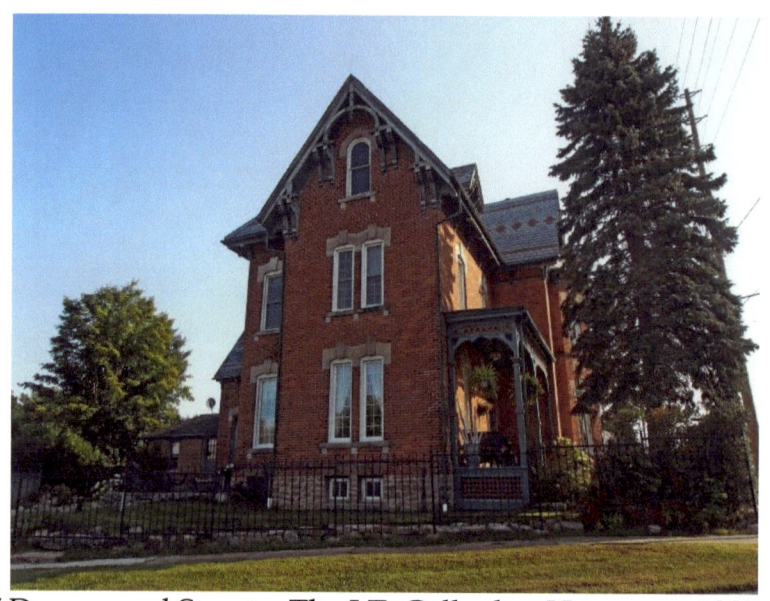

7 Drummond Street – The J.T. Gallagher House – c. 1885 – Gothic Revival style – 2½ storeys tall, 2 storey bay, extensive dripped barge board, locally quarried sandstone lintels; ornate polychromatic slate roof; tall decorative chimneys

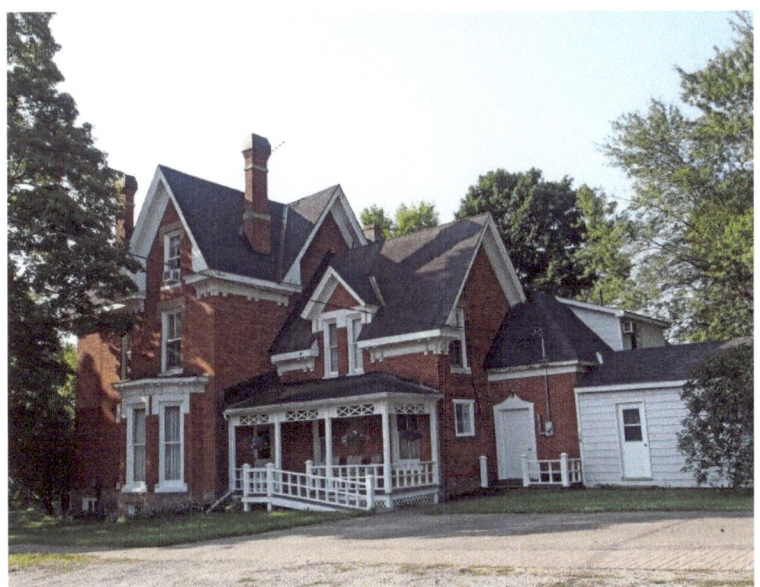

14 By Street – The John Poole Tett House – c. 1896 – Victorian – tall, imposing windows; bay window; cornice brackets

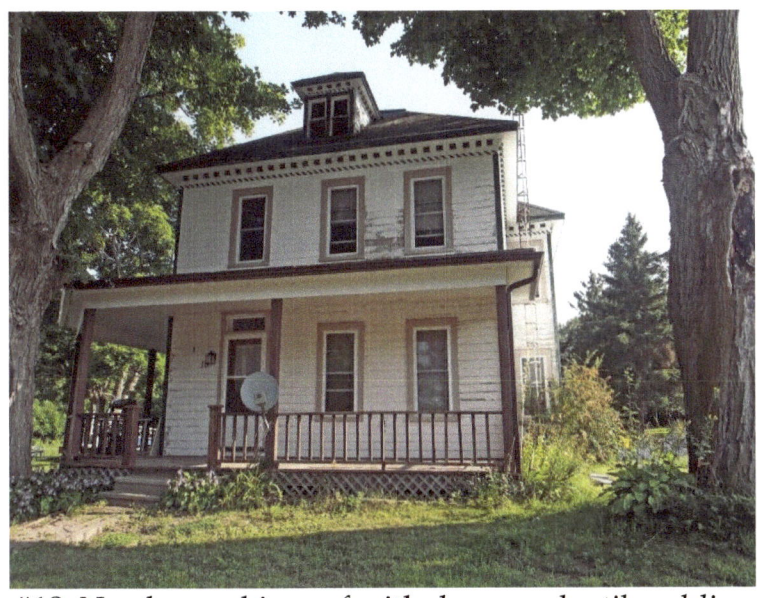

#18, Newboro – hip roof with dormer, dentil molding

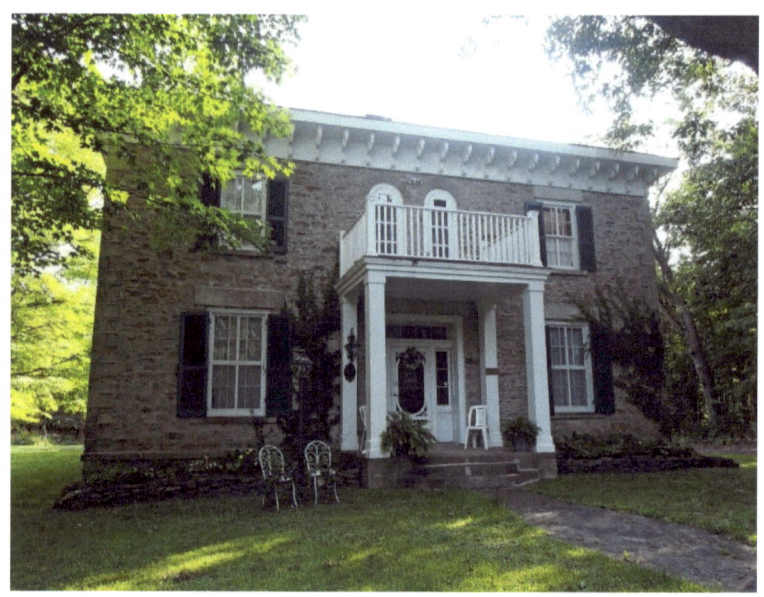

11 New Street – The John Draffin House – c. 1860 – first stone building constructed in Newboro – Italianate – corner quoins with large ashlars; cornice brackets, two round-headed doors opening onto balcony above porch; sidelights and transom – between 1895 and 1945 this was the parsonage for St. Mary's Church

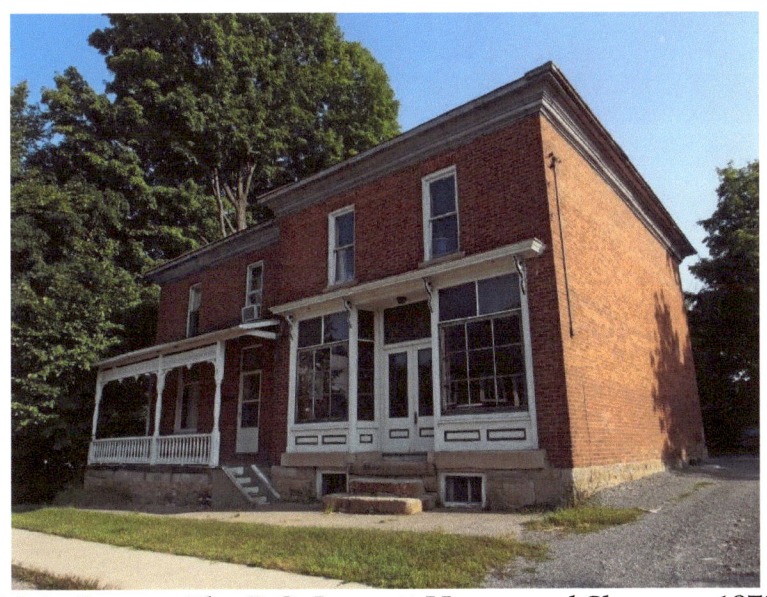

4 Main Street – The R.O. Leggett House and Shop – c. 1870 – furniture and undertaking establishment – intricate treillage work on the veranda posts of the home; large windows of business

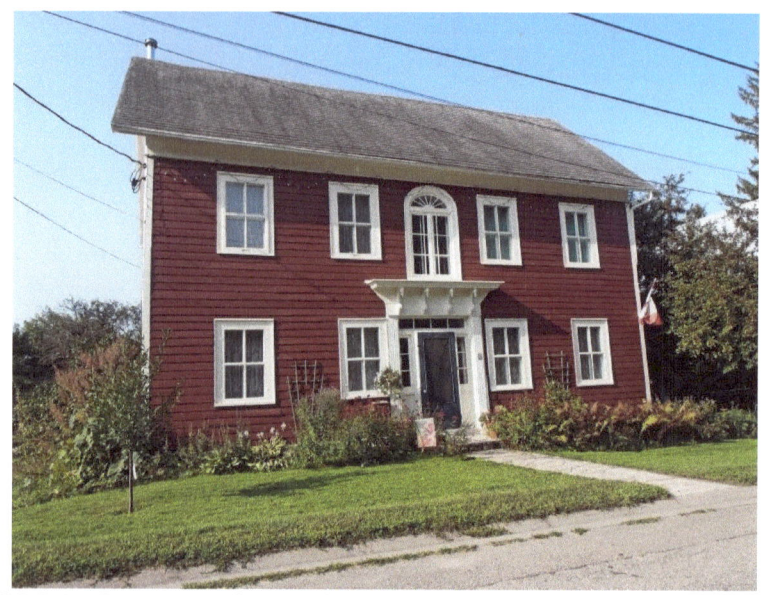

5 Main Street – John Webster House – c. 1860s – Classical Revival style – entrance has a rectangular transom with sidelights to let natural light into the central hallway before there was electricity; bracketed shelf above door; Doric engaged columns flanking the sidelights; central casement window has a fanlight transom above it

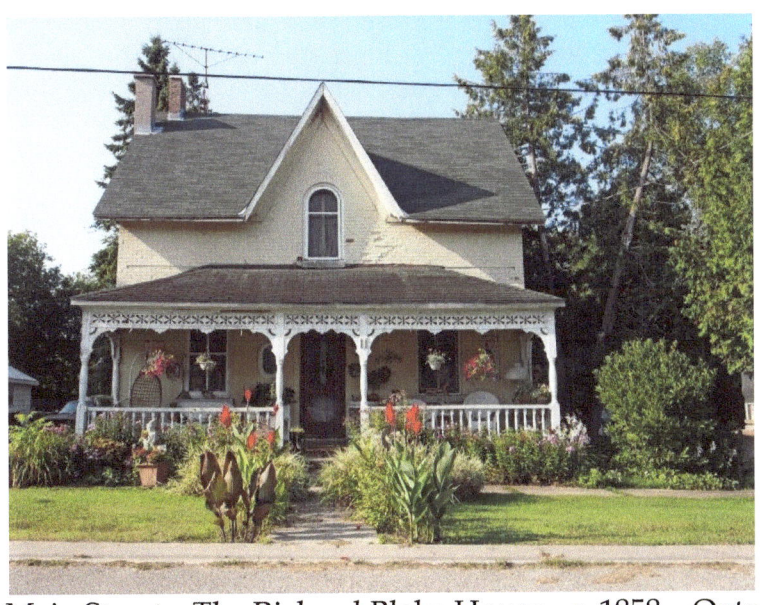

14 Main Street – The Richard Blake House - c. 1858 – Ontario Cottage – 1½ storeys; gable window over front doorway provided light to a central hallway on the upper floor; intricate treillage work on the veranda posts, open railing

Westport and Port Elmsley, Ontario – My Top 5 Picks

Westport

Westport is a village in Eastern Ontario. It lies at the west end of Upper Rideau Lake, at the head of the navigable Rideau Canal system, between Kingston and Ottawa. The first settlers to the Westport area arrived in the period between 1810 and 1820. The land was originally granted by the Crown to a Mr. Hunter, but he never settled in the area and the land was purchased by Reuben Sherwood in 1817. Some of this land was later purchased by the Stoddard and Manhard families. Sawmills built by Sheldon Stoddard and the Manhard brothers in 1828-32, during the construction of the Rideau Canal, fostered the development of Westport. Grist mills and wharves were soon erected and by 1848 a post office was established. Within a decade the hamlet had three hundred residents and several prosperous businesses, including the General Store of Declan Foley and mills of William H. Fredenburgh, a prominent lumber exporter. The community's growth was stimulated by agricultural prosperity and the construction of the Brockville, Westport and Sault Ste. Marie Railway, completed in 1888 between Brockville and Westport, a distance of forty-five miles. With several takeovers, the railway continued to run until 1952.

Port Elmsley

Port Elmsley is located in eastern Ontario in Lanark County on the north shore of the Rideau River between the town of Perth and the town of Smiths Falls.

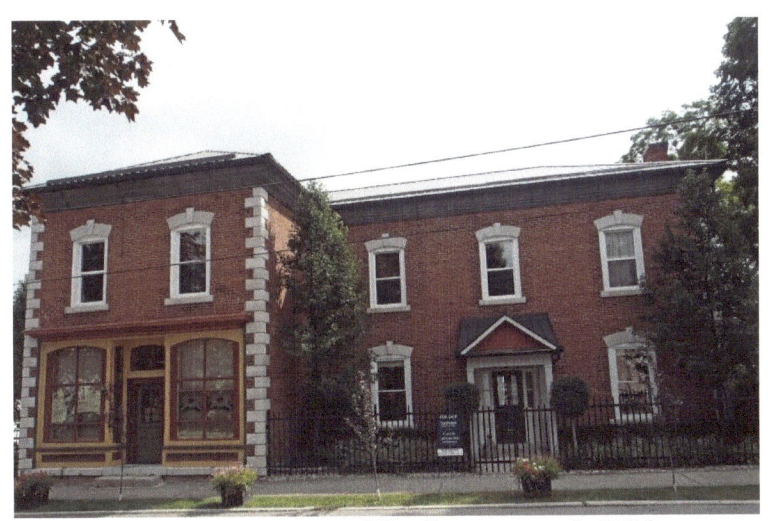

Westport - 45 Main Street - The Prospector's Wife – corner quoins

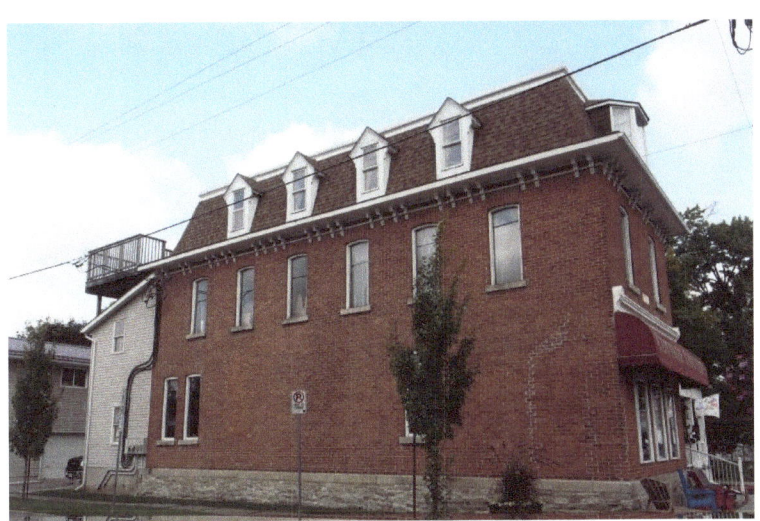

Westport - 18 Church Street – built late 1880s as the home and shop of A.M. Craig, inventor of the one-piece harness buckle; Catholic Women's League Hall from 1921 to 1988; now Cottage Country – mansard roof with dormers

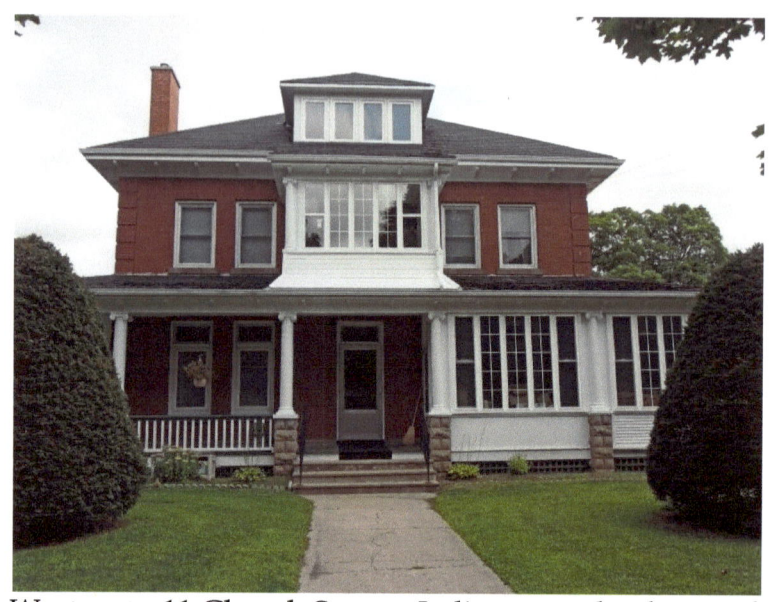

Westport - 11 Church Street - Italianate style - hip roof, dormer, Ionic capitals on verandah pillars

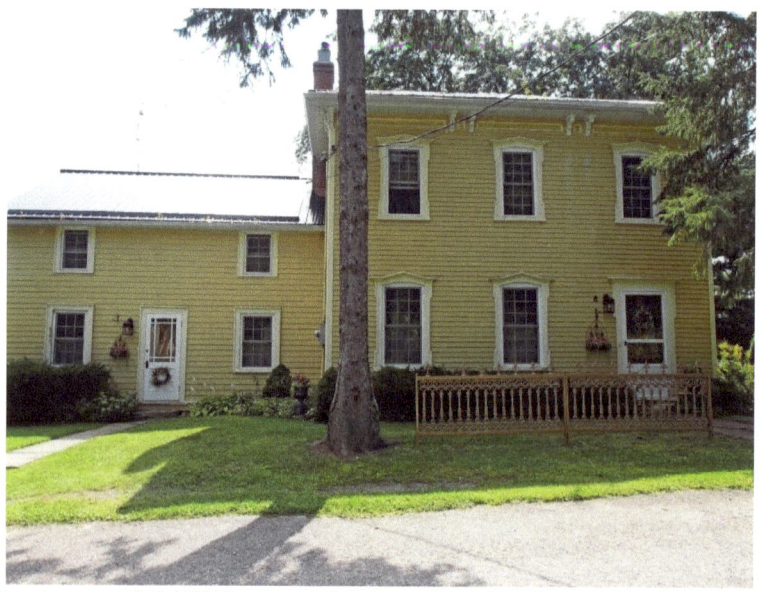

Westport - 8 Mill Street – hip roof, paired cornice brackets, sash windows

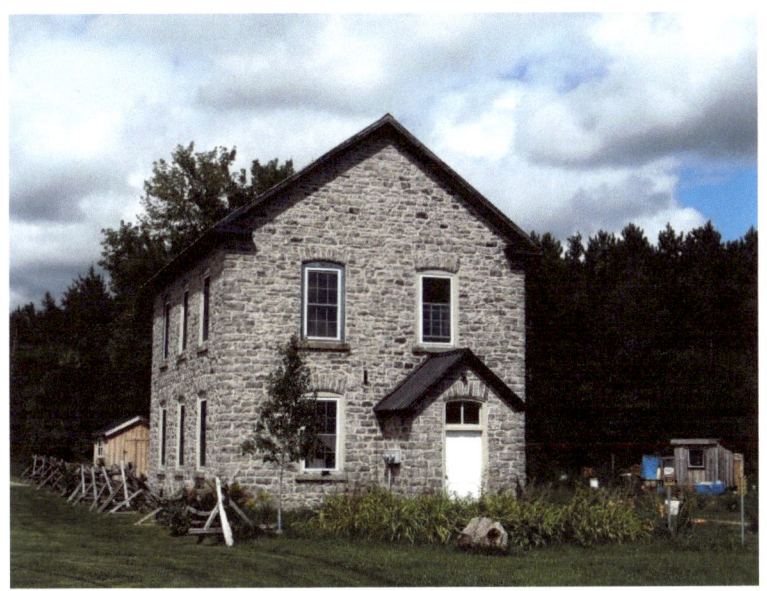

Port Elmsley - cornice return on gable

Perth, Ontario – My Top 15 Picks

Established in 1816, the era when Upper and Lower Canada were British colonies, Perth was one of three strategic defensive outposts created along the Rideau Corridor after the War of 1812. Named after a town and river in Scotland, this small frontier center, located in a large wilderness tract, became the social, judicial and administrative hub for the Scottish and Irish who settled here. Many of the first settlers were military veterans on half pay, while others were military veterans from France, Germany, Poland, Italy, Scotland or Ireland who were offered land in return for their service. The first Scottish settlers came in 1816. Many of the Scottish immigrants were stonemasons; their work can be seen in many area buildings and in the locks of the Rideau Canal.

In 1823, Perth was named the capital of the District of Bathurst, and this attracted a large number of wealthy and educated settlers. When the Rideau Canal was built as a safe inland military route from Kingston to Ottawa between 1826 and 1832, it created a local economic boom. The Tay Canal, from Perth to the Lower Rideau Lake, was first constructed in the 1830s and rebuilt in the 1880s as a commercial waterway. The Tay has become a recreational and tourism area.

The last fatal duel was fought between two young law students on the banks of the Tay River on June 13, 1833, for a lady's honor. In 1892, Perth produced the world's biggest cheddar; it was made from 207,200 pounds of milk and was six feet high, twenty-eight feet in circumference and weighed 22,000 pounds. The mammoth cheese was shipped by train to the Chicago World's Fair the following year.

Perth is the site of the first installation of a telephone other than Bell's experimental installations. A town dentist, Dr. J. F. Kennedy, a friend of Alexander Graham Bell, installed a direct telephone connection between his home and office. By 1887, there were 19 telephones in Perth, with a switchboard in Dr. Kennedy's office.

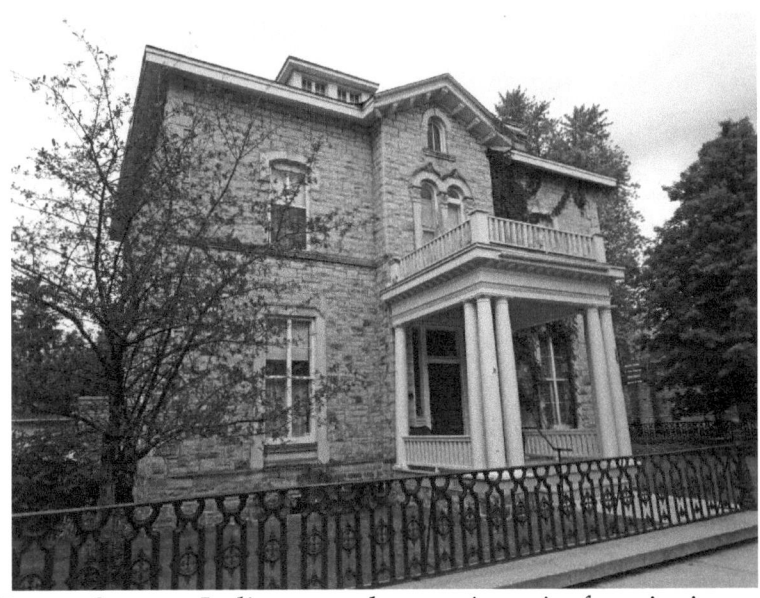

31 Foster Street – Italianate – dormer in attic, frontispiece with decorative window hoods, Doric pillars supporting second floor balconies, tall decorative chimneys

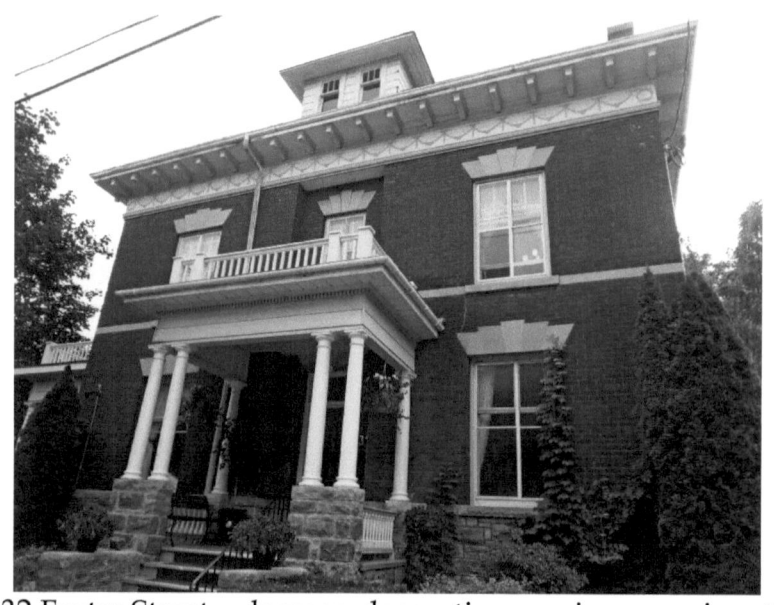

32 Foster Street – dormer, decorative cornice, prominent voussoirs over windows, Doric pillars on stone piers supporting second floor balcony

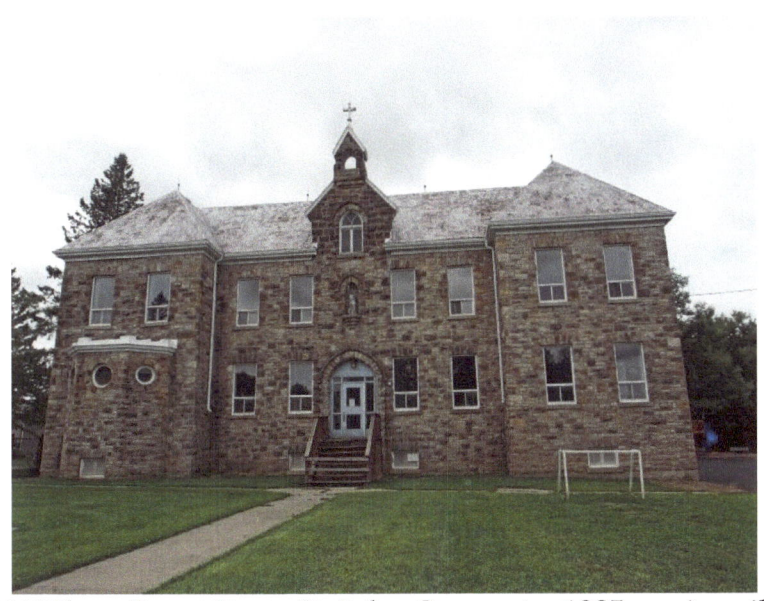

36 Wilson Street East - St. John Convent – 1905 – primarily Gothic with some French Canadian features – stone – center Jacobean gable, bay window with round windows

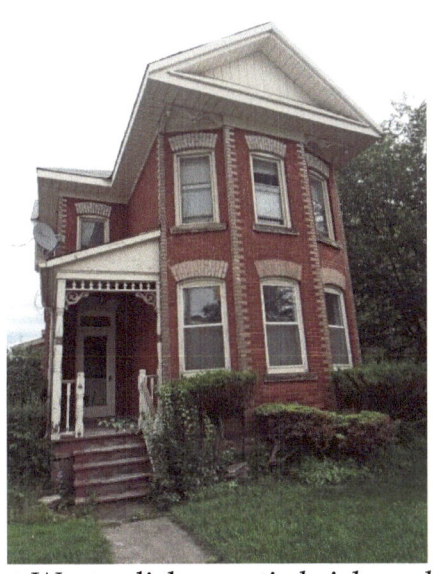

53 Wilson Street West - dichromatic brickwork, spindles and bric-a-brac below porch roof; pediment

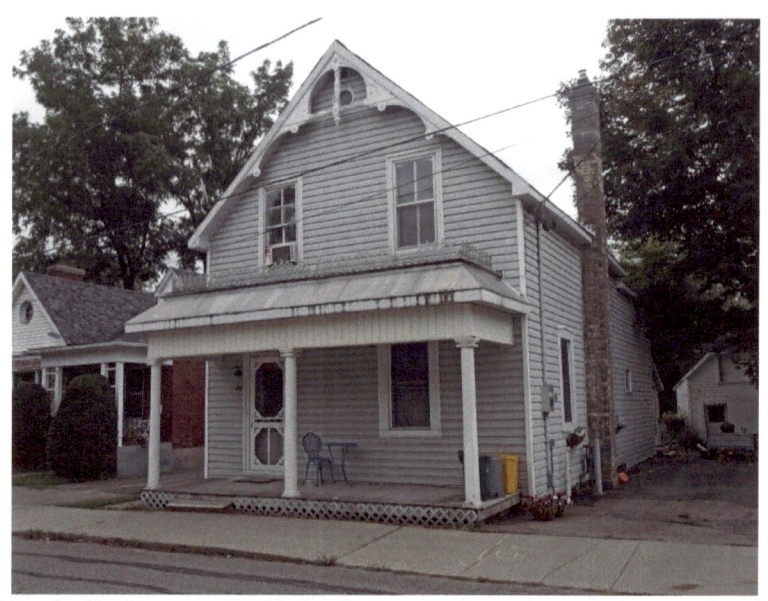

20 Isabella Street - Within the peak is a decorative arch with spindle and stenciling

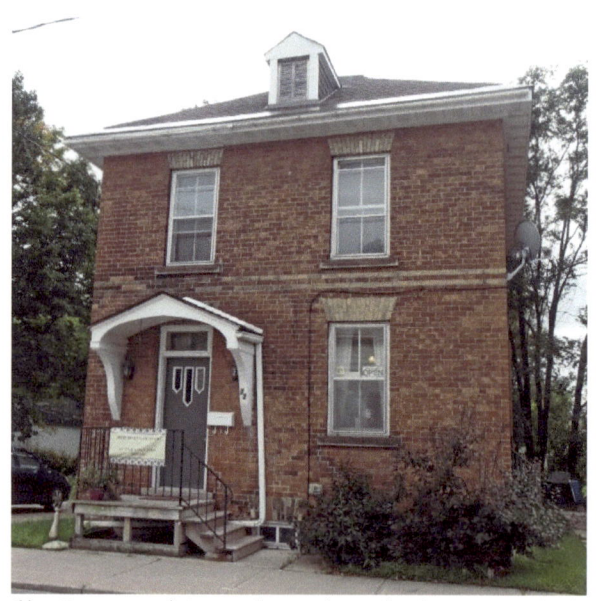

22 Isabella Street – hipped roof with dormer, dichromatic voussoirs and banding

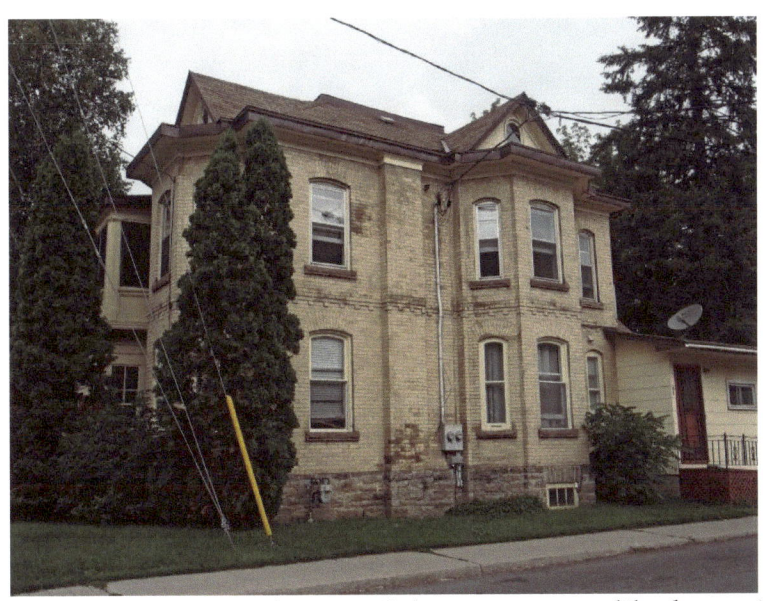

27 Isabella Street – Italianate, 2½ storey tower-like bay with pediment, dentil molding band

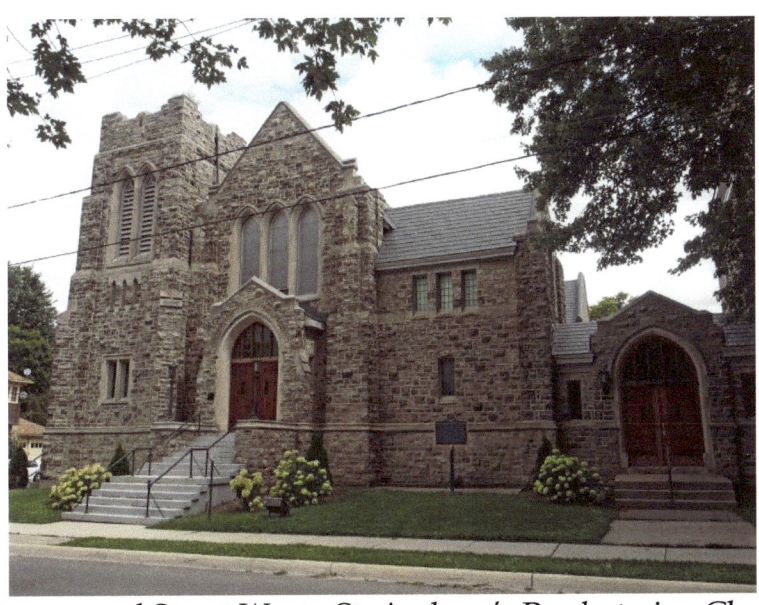

1 Drummond Street West - St. Andrew's Presbyterian Church – built 1832, rebuilt 1898 – Gothic Revival, lancet windows, battlemented tower, buttresses

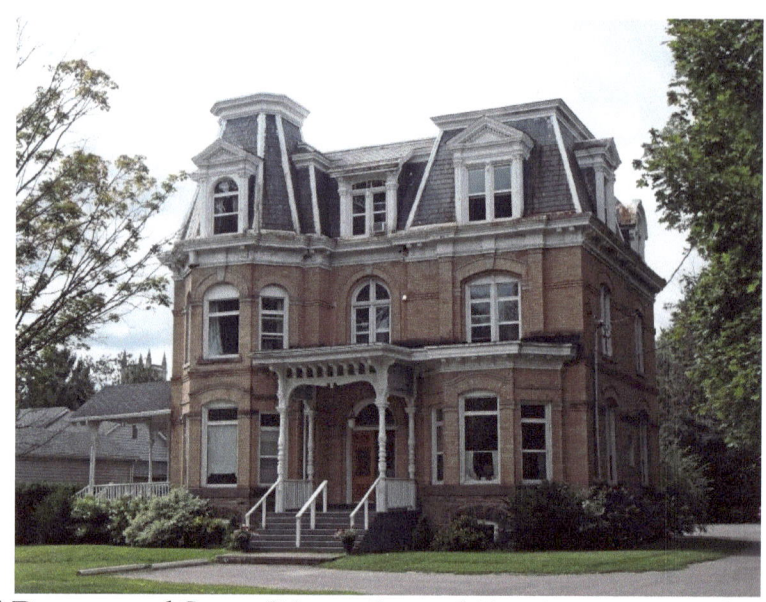

26 Drummond Street West – Second Empire – mansard roof, dormers with window hoods, tower, voussoirs and keystones, turned veranda roof supports with decorative capitals

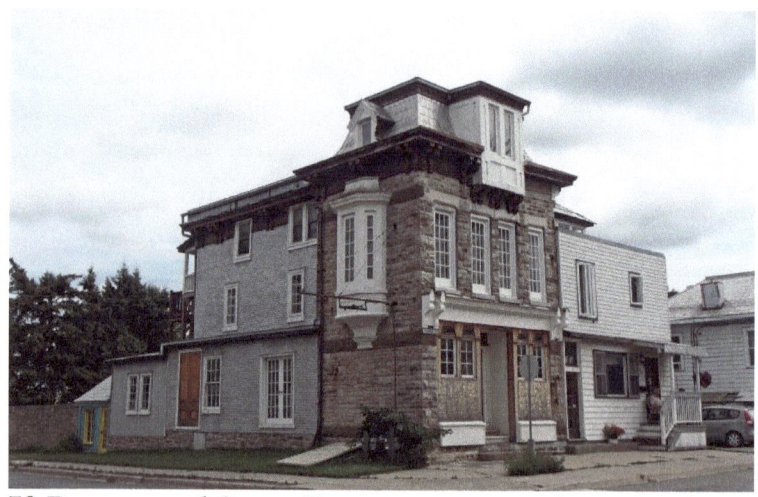

53 Drummond Street East – stone central portion has a mansard-type roof with dormers, oriel window, and cornice brackets

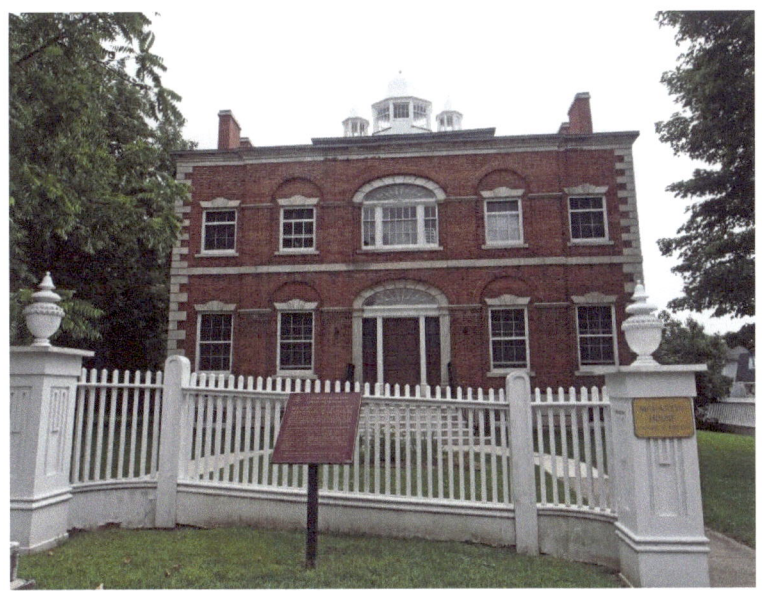

Corner of Gore and Harvey Streets – McMartin House – c. 1831 – erected by United Empire Loyalist descendant, Daniel McMartin, Perth's second lawyer – basic Neo-classical style, and then embellished with unique stylistic features such as recessed arches and a cupola (belvedere) with flanking side lanterns (Federalist style) – widow's walk on roof

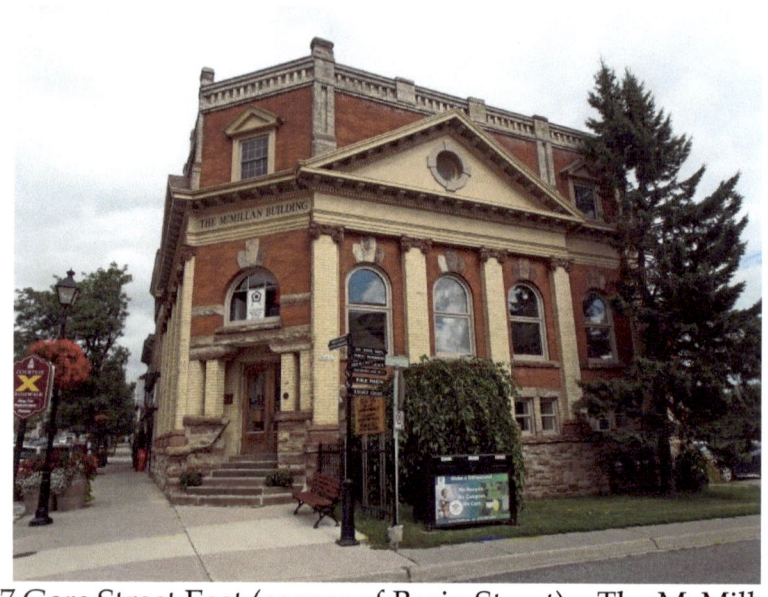

77 Gore Street East (corner of Basin Street) – The McMillan Building – 1907 – former Carnegie Library – Beaux Arts style – pediments, pilasters with composite capitals, elaborate keystones

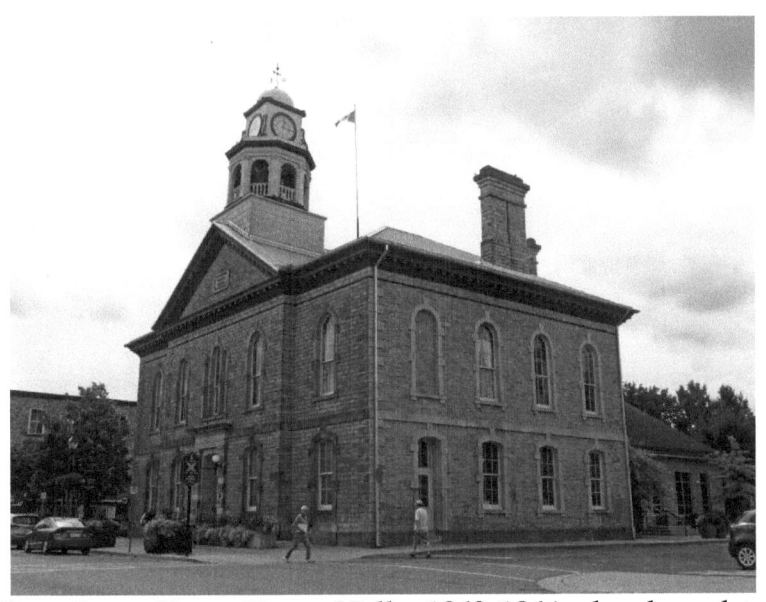

80 Gore Street East – Town Hall – 1863-1864 – local sandstone, frontispiece topped by an elaborate wood cornice, a boxed gable, elaborate bell and clock tower/cupola was added in 1874, architectural detailing in both wood and stone

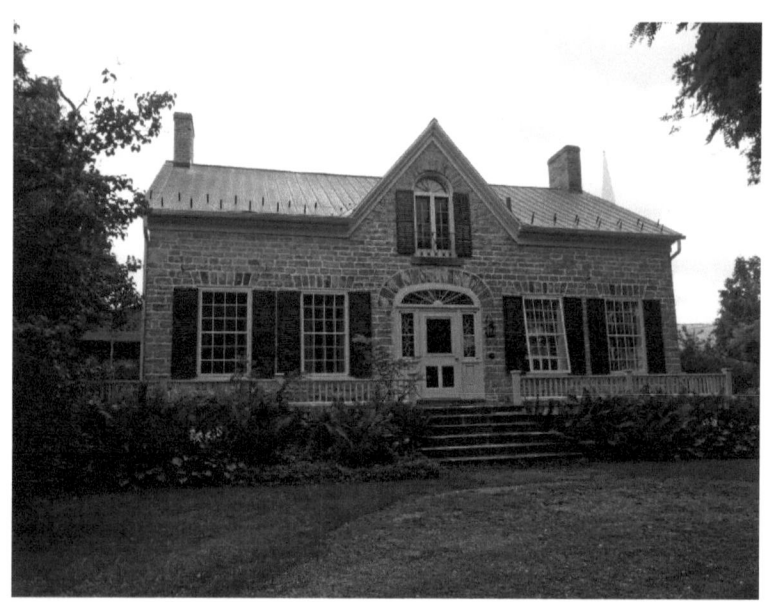

66 Craig Street – Inge-Va (a Tamil word meaning "come here") Museum – local sandstone house – 1824 – Colonial Georgian style of an Ontario cottage – balanced façade, sidelights and transom

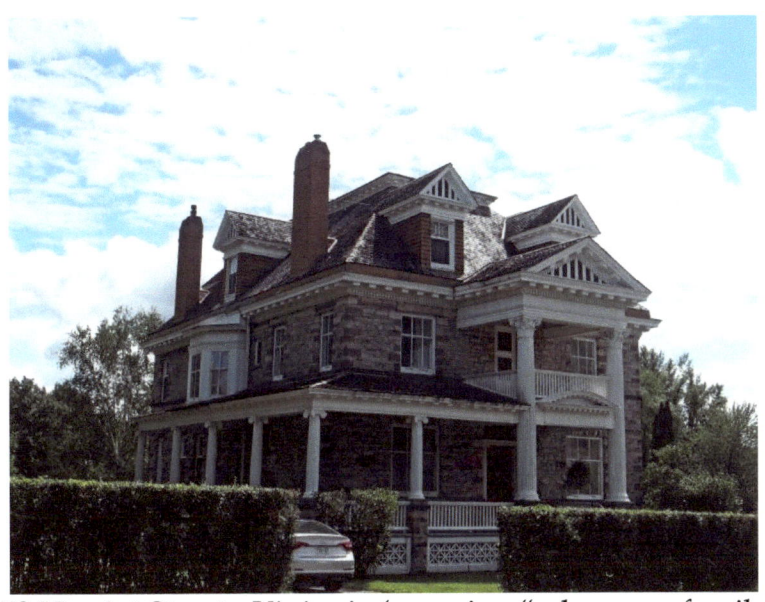

50 Herriot Street - Kininvie (meaning "where my family lives") was built of reddish sandstone in 1906 for textile manufacturer Thomas A. Code – grand Edwardian – said to have been heated by steam from the factory across the street

www.ingramcontent.com/pod-product-compliance
Lightning Source LLC
Chambersburg PA
CBHW040226220526
45473CB00001B/136